DRAWING NEARER
Developing a Mindset of Everyday Worship

Dr. Michael A. Brown

Drawing Nearer
ISBN: 978-0-89098-944-9

©2024 by 21st Century Christian
Nashville, TN 37215
All rights reserved.

All rights reserved. No part of this publication may be reproduced, stored in a retrieval system, or transmitted in any form or by any means—electronic, mechanical, photocopy, recording, digital, or otherwise—without the written permission of the publisher.

Cover design by Jared Kendall

Table of Contents

Chapter 1	What Is Worship?	9
Chapter 2	How Are We to Worship?	27
Chapter 3	Studies in Worship—Cain & Abel	37
Chapter 4	Studies in Worship—Abraham	45
Chapter 5	Studies in Worship—Jacob	53
Chapter 6	Studies in Worship—Nadab & Abihu	63
Chapter 7	Studies in Worship—Saul of Kish	71
Chapter 8	Studies in Worship—David	79
Chapter 9	Studies in Worship—Jeroboam	87
Chapter 10	Studies in Worship—Isaiah	95
Chapter 11	Studies in Worship—Ezra	105
Chapter 12	My Personal Preparation for Worship	115

Author's Note

Worship. It is an overused word. It is a term bantered about in religious circles and often used in a trite or vague manner. Some debate over its meaning, and others grapple with how it should be done. Yet, in spite of this, it is crucial to humanity's very existence. It is a fact that humans will worship and must worship.

Overview

Our approach to this subject is part analytical, part biographical, and part actionable. We will examine pertinent episodes of worship as recorded in Scripture, investigate critical texts concerning worship, and discover key building blocks for developing a greater personal and corporate worship experience.

Each lesson presents practical questions to help the reader take the words off the page and place them into daily life experiences. These are designed to enhance awareness of the presence of God in all of life.

It is my hope that the reader will be challenged and encouraged in developing a mindset of everyday worship that will greatly contribute to the worship experience of the collective gathering of the body of believers.

Chapter One

What is Worship?

Introduction

Have you ever given deeper thought as to what worship is? Though this question can seem almost trite in nature, it is one with which we need to grapple on a personal level. Of course, the great irony in this statement is that we are living in a time where perhaps Christian worship has become more promoted and celebrated than ever before. Drive down any major artery in a town, city, or metropolitan area, and you will see signage promoting a Christian worship in various settings. In today's exploding renaissance of churches, tremendous emphasis is placed upon worship. Seeker-centered churches are promoting praise sessions that are purposely designed to appeal to those seeking to have an experience of God. Familiar music genres are critical to such times of praise. Emotional release is celebrated, and a religious frenzy of sorts is encouraged.

Those who have been disconnected or never connected with "church" engage along with long-time Christians in a sense of connectedness with the Sovereign Lord. However, the question still remains. Is this really what worship is?

The Foundation for Defining Worship

We cannot fully appreciate what worship is without a clear definition. However, a "dictionary" definition will not suffice. We need a definition that lives, moves, and has being. In a sense, we need a definition with some flesh on it if we are going to allow a true worship experience to become incarnate within us. There is no better place for us to begin the process of developing genuine worship than with a focus in Psalms.

Drawing Nearer

Psalms has been described as the hymnbook and/or the prayer book of God's Old Covenant community. The book houses amazing expressions of the human heart's cry to the sovereign God of heaven. Form Criticism, which is the study and analysis of forms of writing, has identified various types or categories of psalms. They break down into hymns, laments, royal psalms, imprecatory psalms, thanksgiving psalms, wisdom psalms, and psalms of ascent. There are a number of different categorizations of the Psalms, and each of them has merit. O. Palmer Robertson's thesis is that the collection can be categorized under the headings of the first two Psalms.[1]

- Heading one (Psalms 1) is the response to God's law by the righteous and the wicked.
- Heading two (Psalms 2) is the establishment of God's Messiah.

Each of the remaining Psalms fits under one of these two header psalms. This approach to Psalms also has merit. However, we need not stress over a particular categorization of the Psalms. Our time is much better spent on recognizing how effective they are in defining what worship is.

It seems that the best place to start in Psalms is with the recognition that each of them reveres the Lord as worthy of whatever they express. Whether it's a hymn of praise, a lament, or a song of a psalm of ascent, the thought conveyed is that the addressee is worthy of being reverently addressed. Our English word *worship* is derived from the Old English *worthscipe*. The variant of this word is *weorthscipe*. Thus we gain the thought of *worthiness*. As we consider the various types of psalms, this thought is clearly borne out.

Hymns

The very mention of the "hymns" puts us in mind of songs sung during a worship service. Some of us come from a church tradition that uses a song to call people together for worship. It is a good way to get Christians to set our minds on the Lord. It

---

[1] *The Structure of the Book of Psalms*, Walter c. Kaiser Jr., Bibliotheca Sacra 174 January-March 2017): 3-12

Chapter One

is also a good way to alert everyone that the set aside time for dedicated focus upon the Lord is commencing. This is a function of this category of Psalms. These psalms are designed to get the attention of the worshipers. They are "focus psalms." They call us from the mundane cares and activities of life to a heavenly focus. They further provide reasons for praising the Lord.

Psalm 92 is an example of a hymn. It begins with a recognition of the appropriateness of giving the Lord thanks and singing praises to His name (Psalm 92:1). Singing praises incorporates giving thanks. One of the more neglected aspects of Christian living is that of giving God thanks for all He does in our lives. Sadly, we live in a time where Christianity is promoted as a system of asking and receiving. Material blessing, financial stability, and the abundance of things are being used as the measure of a blessed life. We, therefore, become unwittingly baptized into the pool of materialism in its many manifestations. Such a mindset skews our thanksgiving to God, because we become tuned into meting out thanksgiving based on whether or not we have acquired "the good life." However, it is good to praise the Lord no matter our situation and circumstances. Like Paul's humble boast to the Christians in Philippi, we can learn to give the Lord thanks in spite of our condition (Philippians 4:11).

The psalmist presented a second focus in this hymn. He focused on an all-day aspect of giving God thanks (Psalm 92:2). From our waking in the morning to our retiring to sleep at night, God's love and faithfulness combine to bind us in blessing. From dawn to dusk, and from dusk to dawn, we experience God's grace. Though we may think that our efforts to live a good life places God under obligation to bless us accordingly, this is not the case. Any good that we receive from the Lord is an act of grace.

This psalmist went on to enumerate reasons for giving God praise (Psalm 92:4-11). He reflected on the ways in which he witnessed God's hand moving in human history. Often, we cannot see the beautiful painting that the Lord is creating until we are pulled further back from the canvas. Verses four and five of this psalm indicate such an experience. Just like Joseph came to see what God was doing during his life history, we can experience times of reflection on what He is doing in ours (Genesis 45:1-8). Upon reflection, we can recognize God's hand in how He vanquishes His enemies while delivering His people (Psalm 92:8-11).

Finally, the psalmist concludes the hymn in the style of the first psalm in the psalter and states the stability and victory of God's people (Psalm 92:12-15). What begins as a call to give God praise ends with a proclamation of praise!

When we think of worshiping God, when we consider drawing nearer to the Lord, the hymns found in the psalter are a great place to start. They can set our minds and hearts right where they need to be. Do you really want to feel the presence of God in a corporate worship gathering?

Then pour through the hymns of Psalms on a regular basis. Read them slowly. Read them reflectively. Ask the Lord to stitch them to your spirit. As the local church family does this as individuals, the opening of our corporate worship will be primed for a new spiritual reality. We will be able to set aside the distractions of life and the tyranny of the urgent. We will be focused on the Lord and on eternity.

Laments

Have you ever reached a point in your Christian walk where you felt the need of a good cry? Have you ever felt a deep sense of defeat and/or sorrow? Have there been times in your Christian experience when you harbored more of a sense of complaining of how your life is going than giving what may be considered artificial praise? The church responded, "AMEN!"

A healthy portion of the psalter consists of laments. As the term indicates, these are psalms addressed to the Lord, which express the frustration of one's experience of life in this world. The laments were scribed out of memories of pain, sorrow, frustration, and angst. However, the laments also include confession of personal sin and thanksgiving and praise for God's goodness and favor. Perhaps laments identify more with our Christian living than do any other in the category of psalms.

Chapter One

A brief examination of Psalm 22 provides us with the basic elements of a lament. As the psalm is examined, one cannot help but see the very words spoken by our Lord while He was living in this world. Jesus was quoting these prophetic words of this psalm while undergoing His crucifixion (Matthew 27:45-50). Although this psalm was written to address a devastating event in the life of the original composer, the words find their ultimate expression in the salvific experience of the Lord.

First, there is the soul-wrenching cry expressing the bewildering, disappointing, and devastating horror of abandonment (Psalm 22:1-2). Though the sense of abandonment is clear, there yet remains the recognition of continued relationship. "My God, My God" expresses the thought of still having union with God but being painfully perplexed as to why He has not interceded on behalf of someone with whom He has a loyal-love covenant relationship.

If we are to be honest about it, we must confess to times in which we have felt that God has abandoned us. Such experiences as the unjust loss of employment, the painful breakup of a marriage, the loss of personal health, or the untimely death of a loved one can evoke a sense of desertion fused with panic. When we have been doing our best to live a faithful, godly life, and we encounter such things, we are often flooded with thoughts of why would God allow such things—especially in our lives. Like Job, we cannot fathom that we would or should be the unwitting victims of such depths of pain. Some even dare to cry out in anger toward God. These are honest expressions of the soul that the lament conveys.

Second, there is a sober and somber recognition of God's power, majesty, and faithfulness. One of the many beautiful facets of the laments is that they refuse to dwell in sorrow. Rather, they ebb and flow with a sense of complaint and hope (Psalm 22:3-5). The psalmist recognized that God is still righteous, holy, and worthy of trust in spite of the current experience of pain and suffering. Much like we experience today, there are those moments within even the deepest grief when we recognize God's sovereignty and goodness. Such times reveal themselves in a spiritual wrestling match between our pain and our hope.

Third, there are the revolving, interwoven thoughts of pain and trouble with hope and trust (Psalm 22:6-21). Though the psalmist clearly saw his condition dire and wretched, he could also reflect in hope of God's mighty deliverance. His belief in God's power and goodness moved him to call upon the Lord in his desperate condition.

Again, we cannot keep ourselves from seeing the striking application of this psalm to the experience of our Lord. It is amazing to see the Holy Spirit's authoring of the Scriptures through human instruments. Whatever personal situation on which the psalmist was reflecting found its ultimate fulfillment in the experience of the Christ.

Finally, the laments abound in praise (Psalm 22:22-31). The composer, having come full-circle in reflection upon his harrowing experience, burst out in shouts of acclamation of God's deliverance. This is the confident hope housed in the hearts of all who steadfastly seek Him and maintain their faith in Him.

The laments serve as somewhat of a spiritual cleansing. They force us to go deeper in our thoughts about the Lord and our relationship with Him. They expose our inward, secret thoughts. They strip us of surface Christianity with its pithy sayings of the "blessed life." Once we are laid bare, they allow us to see God, and see ourselves, much more clearly. We are drawn closer to Him, and the width, breadth, height, and depth of our praise and adoration of Him exponentially increase.

Thanksgiving Psalms

The Scriptures are replete with explosions of thanksgiving. Whether we are reading David's incessant call to thank the Lord or Paul's outbreaks of praise in his letters, God is constantly being thanked. The thanksgiving psalms help us to appreciate the vital importance of giving God thanks. They remind us of His goodness, grace, and mercy, and they prime our pump for personal and corporate worship. They are pregnant with thanksgiving and praise. Psalm 30 is such an example.

Chapter One

The composer begins this psalm with reflection upon an experience of God's deliverance from deadly peril (Psalm 30:1-3). As stated earlier, the psalter contains compositions reflecting on previous experiences with the Lord. Whether little or much time had elapsed between the act of deliverance and the time of composition cannot be fully determined. Regardless, the experience itself was very much alive in the heart of the writer.

It is helpful to compare psalms of lament with psalms of praise. In the case of Psalm 30, the composer declares his deliverance as a result of his cry to the Lord. He indicates no delay in this deliverance—as opposed to what is expressed in a lament. Of course, there might have been a delay, but the writer only focused on the deliverance (Psalm 30:1-3).

Thanksgiving psalms implore God's people to join in the praise (Psalm 30:4). What began as an individual declaration of intent quickly moved to a call to others to participate. This serves as a powerful lesson for our corporate worship experiences. It speaks to the importance of preparation by those that would lead us in the worship experience. In some instances, the song leader, praise director, or minister of music (or whichever terminology is used) brings no sense of praise or thanksgiving to the task. No personal life experience has moved him so as to stir him to call others to praise the Lord along with him. Conversely, a lack of recognition of heaven's involvement in the experience of the congregants may stifle the spirit of the song leader and dissuade him from pouring his heart out in thanksgiving to the Lord. Either scenario can be detrimental to our drawing nearer to the Lord.

Psalm 30 goes on to provide some insights as to the composer's situation. In this case, there was a time of supposed self-sufficiency, which was painfully exposed for its fallaciousness (Psalm 30:6-10). The psalmist, having been summarily humbled by the loss of God's favor, greatly rejoiced in the restoration of this favor (Psalm 30:11-12). His praise and thanks could never again be quenched. God had delivered him, and he well knew it. His thanks would continue throughout his life.

There can be no drawing closer to the Lord without a heart of thanksgiving. It is often a lack of thanksgiving that prevents us from truthful and spiritual worship experience. Sadly, some approach the Lord with a sense that they are *owed* by God rather than *owned* by God (Luke 17:1-6). Such a spirit prohibits the worship experience.

There is also the danger of approaching God with a "slot-machine" mentality. This is the person who thinks of the Lord as granting blessing in response to something we give to Him. God cannot be connived or bought. Our good thoughts, words, or deeds never earn us His favor. Though the Scriptures reveal a God who rewards the pure-motive obedient, the reward is always a gracious one. Thanksgiving psalms reflect the grateful heart of the worshiper honoring the God who owes no good thing to His fallen creation, yet He gave the greatest gift ever: He gave His Son (John 3:16).

Wisdom Psalms

Wisdom is an oft-used word. We must immediately qualify what we mean when we speak of wisdom. There is the wisdom of the world. This is seeded in the thoughts of humankind. It is focused on getting the best out of life "under the sun." It is the counsel centered in living in a two-dimensional plan as if that is all that there is. No consideration is given to the larger reality. The three-dimensional plan, the heavenly dimension is absent. God is not acknowledged, and the requirement of giving an account for how one behaves in this world is ignored (Ecclesiastes 12:13-14). Solomon warned us of the emptiness of this approach to life [long ago] (Ecclesiastes 1:1-14). Worldly wisdom leads to eternal death.

As opposed to worldly wisdom, the wisdom psalms promote God's view of how life should be lived under the sun. They speak of a life that is truly worth living. Since the God of heaven created human life, since He fashioned the realm of human life, and since He controls the sphere of human life, it only makes sense that we should follow His counsel in and throughout life. We are only

Chapter One

wise when we operate in this world in the way that our Creator directs. When God chose Israel as His Old Covenant people, His directive and His plea was that they would choose life as opposed to death (Deuteronomy 30:15-20). The wisdom psalms work with this same dynamic. They present to us the path of life and of death. They tell us the end of our choice as we stand at the beginning of our choice.

The first psalm in the psalter is a powerful example of a Wisdom Psalm. The opening salvo is stated in a congratulatory manner, descriptive of the God-follower's station in life. It is a "blessed" state (Psalm 1:1). The word *blessed* describes a person in an enviable position. It is someone in whose position you would want to be. The word also suggests one, who because of his state, is worth congratulating. This person is not "lucky," which implies "chance." Rather, he is genuinely the recipient of God's favor. Such favor is not found in an abundance of transient material things or with the fame and fortune offered by this world. God's abiding presence rests with Him, and this far outweighs anything that the things of time could offer.

This wisdom psalm presents three key reasons undergirding this person's blessed status and three types of persons from which this person turned away. Wisdom psalms reveal that being blessed is a matter of choice—not chance. This life is described as blessed because he chose how to think, how to behave, and with whom to keep company, and his choice was based upon having a close relationship with God (Psalm 1:1-2). The result of such decisions is a stable life. It is a life that can be described as solid. It is not that this life is absent from struggle. However, even in the midst of mighty storms, he stands firm. It is a fruitful, productive life. Unlike a withered, rotted and unstable tree, he is always in full life, full leaf, and full fruit. It is a prosperous life. We must understand prosperity in a broader sense than that which is material. Prosperity can be a peaceful home and good health (Psalm 1:3). Like God presented to Israel of old, the wisdom psalms present the path of true life. They serve as a means of genuinely getting the best out of life in this world.

Drawing Nearer

The wisdom psalms also present the alternative to the blessed life (Psalm 1:4-6). There is a drastic difference. There is instability and fragility in their existence. They are rootless and bound for a certain judgment of condemnation. Following the counsel of other fallen humans, imitating the behavior of those in rebellion against the Lord and keeping in union with those who scorn the very nature of a God-fearing life lead to their utter destruction.

Many science fiction movies explore the notion of having a second chance in life. These present some manner in which an individual can go back into the past and make changes that positively impact their future. Admittedly, these are popular and entertaining for good reason. Rarely would anyone refuse the opportunity to magically go back in life and correct wrong decisions and moves. Human lives are lived in imperfection, and regrets grow up like weeds in the field. Thanks be to God for His forgiveness of our foolish ways. However, the wisdom psalms are designed to prevent us from much heartache in life. They allow us to see the full picture from the start. We are wise to heed them and thus save ourselves the drama of life.

The grace of God is also meted out via the wisdom psalms. This is realized when we come to these psalms having already chosen the wrong path in life. The grace is seen in that we can choose to change. Thank God that we do not have to continue to drudge along in a miserable life because of bad choices we made in the past. We can decide to start sowing better seeds so that we can begin to reap a better harvest. Further, we can lean on God's grace to sustain us while reaping a bad harvest because of past wrong choices.

When we consider all these elements of wisdom psalms, they can greatly contribute to our worship. We are moved to give God praise for showing us the path to a life worth living. We are moved to give God mighty thanks for His mercy shown in allowing us to turn to a better way. We can marvel in praise that we may not yet be where these psalms call us to be, but we are no longer aimlessly toiling in the unwise path that we once trod. An assembly of people so focused lifts our worship to heights and depths that keep us moving closer and closer to our Lord.

Chapter One

Imprecatory Psalms

To *imprecate* is to invoke or to call down against someone. Therefore, an Imprecatory Psalm is one that calls for others to be cursed for their oppressive sins. Such psalms may seem out of step with the heart of God-followers and out of step with the Lord Himself. Even today, some consider such psalms as incongruent with being a Christian. Yet, the psalter contains several such psalms.

To better understand and appreciate these psalms, we must reach beyond our platitudes and strip ourselves of all facades of displaying Christian love. We must force ourselves to look at our raw feelings when confronted with injustices. As with the laments, these psalms require a look at how we feel and even express our feelings of anger when no one is looking or listening. It is us behind closed doors.

Psalm 10 is an example of an Imprecatory Psalm. The psalm opens with a cry to the Lord against the heartless, domineering, and shamelessly abusive treatment of an oppressor. These psalms cry out in distress—imploring the Lord to provide deliverance from blatant injustice (Psalm 10:1-11). The Imprecatory Psalm decries the utter disdain shown by those who commit such acts of injustice and calls upon the Lord to right these unconscionable wrongs. The spirit of the composer cannot conceive of the righteous God allowing these abuses to continue. Justice must prevail. The oppressor must be judged. The blasphemer must be silenced. The belligerent sinner must be condemned. The innocent must be avenged. Yet, this psalm expresses the pain of a somewhat disappointed faith: "Why has the Lord not yet acted on behalf of the suffering?" Still, there is the boldness to appeal to the Lord to act in justice (Psalm 10:12-13), and there is confident assertion that justice will be done (Psalm 10:14-15).

The Imprecatory Psalms include praise and thanksgiving as well. The composer of Psalm 10 conveys thoughts of both (Psalm 10:16-18). The situation may be dire, the earnest plea for help may be temporarily delayed, but the sureness of God's deliverance can be absolute. It is because of these eternal truths that the psalmist gave God praise for what he confidently expected. If we read these psalms from the standpoint of the composer's reflection on past experiences, we can picture him having come to even greater confidence in the fact that the judge of the entire world would always do what is right.

The cry of this psalm is ageless. In every era of human history, there have been those who wanted to impose their wicked wills upon others. They have no conscience regarding the pain they inflict. Some take pleasure in doling out such pain. Worse, they seem to oppress with impunity. Still worse is the fact that many have done so while upholding a Christian banner! In families, in communities, in politics, in governments, in national crisis, and in international conflict, history has seen this scene play out. We should expect such scenes to continue to play out until the Lord returns to judge this world in righteousness (Acts 17:31).

The value of such psalms to our personal lives cannot be minimized. We often find ourselves in circumstances that wreak havoc on our faith. Sometimes, these come in the form of relationships. Sadly, for example, some Christians enter relationships that become emotionally, verbally, or even physically abusive. The innocent party often suffers silently for fear of reprisals. Earnest prayers are offered, yet there is seemingly no deliverance in sight.

Times of sickness and the death of loved ones can cause tremendous strain on our faith. This is particularly true when we deem it unfair. A woman unexposed to cancer risks is still diagnosed with it. A man is killed when struck by a drunk driver. A child is stricken by a genetic disease. Each case makes us wonder why this has happened. Each situation forces us to cry out in sadness and frustration. Each causes us to have a Job-like period during which time we struggle with God.

Experiencing injustice can take a toll on our faith. We can become the victims of criminal activity, employer/employee mistreatment, and even damaging government policy. We can find ourselves being taken advantage of by powers and authorities against which we have no ability to fight. These circumstances can wreck our lives and shipwreck our faith.

The devil uses all such conditions to place a wedge between us and God. He wants to convince us that God cannot be counted on, has no ability to change, and/or cares nothing about our plight. However, Imprecatory Psalms can help us overcome such circumstances. They remind us of God's righteousness, omnipotence, omniscience, and omnipresence. They teach us of His ultimate deliverance for His children.

The corporate value of these psalms is immeasurable. When we come together to worship our God, we give voice to the various struggles and strains that we have been under by means of our songs to Him. Pain meets with praise, and the two combine in a symphony of glorifying, life-experiencing, and faith-affirming song. The spiritual body is edified, and the local church's mindset and worldview are reset as the body of Christ prepares to face another week.

Royal Psalms

The term *royal* quickly impresses the mind with thoughts of kingship. This is an accurate picture, because these psalms are focused on God's sovereignty. They proclaim and celebrate the rule of God over all that is, was, and shall be. Psalm 24 is an example of these types of psalms.

Royal Psalms properly position the Creator in relation to His creation. They present the Lord as He is—high and lifted up and sovereign over all that is, was, and shall be. They leave no doubt as to God's rule. In addition to this, they boldly state that it is in the Lord's purview, and only in His purview, that blessing and favor come to His creation. In this particular psalm, the holiness and righteousness of God are declared along with what is required to come into His presence (Psalm 24:3-6). Further, the tremendous benefits of His presence are declared for those who would prepare themselves to meet Him (Psalms 24:7-10).

The power of the Royal Psalms is seen in that they allow us to keep the unpredictability and uncertainty in life in proper perspective. Whatever be the source of our angst, believing in and accepting God's sovereignty keeps our feet settled and our hearts secure. We don't have to live in this world as victims of chance or fate. This world often appears to be on a meandering, chaotic course with no particular end in sight, but the Royal Psalms present a completely different reality. This world and time itself are in the hands of the righteous God who is ultimately leading it to judgment. He finds and accepts those who seek Him. They praise Him for His righteousness, mercy, and power. They welcome His coming.

Royal Psalms enable our personal lives to keep perspective. They still our hearts in the worst of circumstances. They settle our souls in times of despair. They keep our minds sure in times of doubt. All of this can mightily contribute to our times of corporate praise. We can sing, "It is Well with My Soul" with a greater sense of security. Such times of praise allow us to face this world with a tenacity of faith that will not soon wilt under the pressures and trials of this life.

Ascent Psalms

Have you ever had a song on your heart while traveling? This may have occurred while driving to a vacation destination or heading out to see some exciting event. Whichever the case, you doubtless sang with the joy of the anticipation of reaching your destination. This is the thought behind Ascent Psalms.

Scholars have placed these psalms in the context of God's people going up to worship Him. Geographically speaking, Jerusalem was on higher ground and required traveling upwards to reach the temple. In contemporary times, the applicable thought is that of going up to meet with the Lord. Whether we think of this from a historic geographical perspective or from a moral or even a spiritual perspective, worship is always about reaching higher.

Psalm 122 is a quintessential Ascent Psalm. The composer's opening words express the joy of an opportunity to come to God's house (Psalm 122:1). There is an added sense of anticipation that something good is going to come from this experience. There is a heart of gratitude for being able to go to God's house. All

Chapter One

of this is buttressed by a belief in God's power and presence to be experienced in His house. A sad historical note is that Israel saw this hope dashed at the sacking of the city and the burning of the temple by the Babylonians (2 Chronicles 36:15-21). The subsequent effort to rebuild this earthly representation of God's house (535 B.C.) met with further disappointment among some (Ezra 3:12-13). The last attempt proved to be devastating (70 A.D.). However, eschatologically speaking, the real house of God has never and will never be shaken. For Christians today, this is the house of the Lord to which this psalm ultimately points. We enjoy a foretaste of it in time as we make our pilgrimage to eternity.

This psalm speaks to the common goal of a united people of God (Psalm 122:4). The twelve tribes of Israel find common purpose in ascending to Jerusalem to give God praise. Again, the historical reality is not pleasant to remember. After David's death, Solomon's heart was turned from following the true God to following false gods (1 Kings 11:4-12). This resulted in the split of the kingdom in the days of Solomon's son, Rehoboam (1 Kings 12:1-24) and the deeper levels of corruption introduced by Jeroboam (1 Kings 12:25-33). Christians can and should learn from this appalling past and do all we can to become a united body of believers seeking to give life praises to the Lord.

This psalm culminates with a call to pray for the total well-being of God's city (Psalm 122:6-9). Envisioned here is the welfare of God's people. Peace and prosperity speak to the total life experience of a people kept by the Lord in conditions that make for the best of what is truly important in life. The composer urged that all of God's people would join in unison toward this reality. Again, historically speaking, such a state was never sustained. The glory years of David's rule provided a glimpse of this reality. However, as a result of his sin with Bathsheba and Uriah, the nation entered into a downward spiral from which it never fully recovered (2 Samuel 11:1—12:15). Thankfully, this was not the end of the story. Because of God's grace, His great love of Israel, and His faithfulness to His covenantal promises, Christians today look forward to the full experience of the eternal rest, peace, and prosperity that we will share in together with the Lord. We will enjoy the unending reality of being in the ultimate house of God where wars cannot exist and peace cannot be extinguished.

As with the other genres of psalms, there is definitely a place for Ascent Psalms in our personal lives and in the life of the local church. Individually, we can ask the Lord to set our minds on the blessing of coming into His house each week. As we practice the discipline of our spirit to think toward this end, the Holy Spirit works with us to think of our times of worship as a foretaste of what eternity will be like. Of course, this requires that we not dwell on the imperfections of other Christians. Such imperfections often lead to gossip, back-biting, and other unity-destroying mindsets. These are easy for us to see in others. However, the reality is that the avoidance of the negatives often found in spiritual body life begin with self-examination. Interestingly enough, the more we allow the Spirit to work within us, the less we see of those behaviors that erode Christian unity. As goes the old song, we are really the ones that stand in the need of prayer.

Corporately, the Ascent Psalms can be employed to help set the tone of our worship. They can be used as calls to worship. They can be creatively promoted during the week in preparation for worship. A variety of means can be used to prepare members daily for the meeting time ahead. All of this can make for a spiritual body that is prepared to come to the foot of the holy mountain to meet with the Holy One.

Final Thoughts

The various genres of psalms really sit at the heart of our personal and public worship. When regularly read, studied, and meditated upon, they serve to strip us bare before the Lord. They allow us to communicate with Him in transparency. We grow to the point that we are naked before Him, yet we are without shame. It is not that we somehow reach sinless perfection by means of delving

Chapter One

ourselves into the psalms. Much the opposite is true. We, in our fallenness, draw closer to the throne of grace. Our closet-time before the Lord becomes a more comfortable place as we express our hearts to Him in sincerity and with complete transparency. The result is the development of a much closer walk with the Father of mercies and the subsequent rise of a fountain of praise for who He is and what He has done. May we as individual Christians and as the local church use these spiritual gems to prepare us for worshiping our God.

For Further Thought

1. Think of a "reflection moment" that you have had. What did it reveal to you about God's hand in your life?
2. What are some practical ways in which song and praise leaders and congregants can best help one another prepare for corporate times of worship?
3. Why is the thought of a gracious reward often difficult for us to grasp?
4. How can the Wisdom Psalms minister to the unchurched as well as the churched people?
5. What personal experience have you had that is fitting of an Imprecatory Psalm?
6. What are some creative ways that the local church can make use of Ascent Psalms?
7. Which genre of the psalms most consistently touches your heart? Why?
8. How can you use Psalms to develop yourself spiritually?

Drawing Nearer

Chapter Two

How Are We to Worship?

Introduction

As we learned in the opening lesson, the entirety of Christian life is designed to be centered in worship (Romans 12:1-2). This takes worship beyond the sphere of what we do on Sundays and gets more into what we do every day. However, we do need to concern ourselves with how we are to worship as a local church. What is appropriate or inappropriate? Who decides this? How is it decided? Let us turn our attention to this matter.

A Brief Historical Overview

Whenever Christians encounter questions regarding worship, we cannot afford to ignore the past. We must begin with the recognition that we are not the first Christ-followers to ask these questions. This same principle applies to practically all aspects of Christian life and practice. It seems that every generation of Christians has had to wrestle with questions as to how to faithfully follow the Lord in their given era.

At the core of deciding how we are to worship the Lord is our approach to the Bible. Our thoughts and our attitudes about the Holy Scriptures greatly determine what we believe and how we practice our faith. However, things are a bit more complicated than this. The fact is that the world has tremendous influence over even our thoughts about the Bible.

Drawing Nearer

Generally speaking, Christian viewpoints on the Bible have often been influenced by the popular thinking of a given era. Philosophy and other social sciences (soft sciences) are involved in the categorization and evaluation of how people view the world in various time periods. Broadly speaking, we can observe three major eras of thought: Premodernism (from the beginning up to the 1650s), Modernism (1650s to 1950s), and Postmodernism (1950s to today). Each era has impacted our viewpoint on the Bible. In Premodernism, the common view was that there is ultimate divine authority, absolute truth, and a final source of that truth. For Christians, this is the acknowledgment of God and the Holy Scriptures.

In the era of Modernism, science was looked at as the means of determining truth. Only that which is measurable and explainable by experimentation and human reasoning can be qualified as truth. The Bible came to be suspect in part—particularly where its message could not be rationally explained or scientifically verified.

In the present era of Postmodernism, the previous two era's conclusions are both suspect. The idea of an ultimate source of authority, and the acceptance of the notion of absolute truth, are largely dismissed. The individual is sovereign. A person's thoughts on what is true trump any thoughts to the contrary. The notion of a spiritual, moral, or ethical standard to which all persons must be accountable is laughable at best.

The foregoing is a general categorization. A detailed analysis would involve a discussion on the classical Greek philosophers, the enlightenment period, rationalism, empiricism, and the many related and opposing philosophical systems. However, this general view helps us in wrestling with the question of how we are to worship the Lord. This is true because these various schools of thought impact how we approach the Bible. Do we accept it as the infallible, authoritative Word of God sufficient for instruction on who the Lord is, what He has done, and how we are to respond to Him? Do we consider it as part of a cadre or conglomeration of sources that we need to draw closer to God?

Chapter Two

Is it really a message from God, or is it a collection of things that people merely understood God to be saying?

For those who accept it as the authoritative Word of God, the questions go more in the direction of how we are to use it. Here, we encounter matters of hermeneutics, theology, and contextualization. It can become so complicated of a discussion, and many choose to avoid all such matters and simply follow the church traditions to which they are accustomed.

As Christians, we are best served to accept the Scriptures as the complete, Spirit-inspired, inerrant Word of God that is sufficient and efficient in guiding us in what to believe, how to worship God, and how to live in response to God's call upon our lives (2 Timothy 3:15-17). In addition, we are best served to look for clear indications for how God instructed and guided His old and new covenant people in these and in related areas.

Further, seeking to apply the principles driving those prescribed behaviors within our current-day context is in order. Finally, a safe mantra from which to operate is that if God were honored by the patterns and behaviors prescribed for worship and daily living among the early Christians, then we should seek to follow these as best we can in our time. Though everything from an ancient error cannot be replicated across centuries, certainly the principles behind them can be. This is a God-honoring approach for how we should worship and live for the Lord.

Worshiping Our God

It seems that the matter of how we are to worship the Lord has long been controversial. Students of the Old Testament can quickly bring to mind the various instances where God demanded His worship to be unique. For example, in a time of rampant paganism, God demanded that He not be worshiped like the pagan gods (Deuteronomy 12:1-4; 29-32). Biblical historians and archaeologists have unearthed a wealth of information concerning the worship of pagan gods.

Much of this information describes illicit sexual acts, physical maiming, and child sacrifice—all in the name of worship.

Drawing Nearer

Canaanite religion was replete with such detestable practices, and God forbade His people from joining in or replicating these pagan rituals. Whether it be worship of Baal or Ashtoreth, or the sacrificing of their children to Molech, or obeisance (homage) to the demands of Chemosh, God's people were to reject it all (Leviticus 20:1-5; 1 Kings 11:1-8).

The Scriptures present another striking case on how God's people had to approach Him carefully as opposed to doing so in any manner that they chose. When David sought to transport the Ark of God from where it had been taken and return it to its rightful place, a tragedy occurred (2 Samuel 6:1-11). A man named Uzzah reached out to steady the ark. He was instantly put to death. Only the Levites were to carry the ark, and they had to do so in a specified manor (Exodus 25:12-15; Numbers 4:5-6, 15). Later, the king sought again to bring the ark to its rightful place. However, this time, he was careful to follow God's instruction in detail (1 Chronicles 15:1-15).

The point to be made is that when God gives instructions about man's approach to Him, these cannot be ignored with impunity.

In addition to speaking of what should not be done in worship, the Lord God gave instruction on what should be done in worship and where it was to be done (Deuteronomy 12:5-28). King Hezekiah (2 Chronicles 29-31), and even more strikingly, King Josiah (2 Chronicles 34-35) have gone down in the annals of Israel's history as good kings who restored the worship of the Lord in accordance with His instructions. The case of Josiah is particularly noteworthy in that his reforms were an immediate reaction to the finding of the Book of Law, which contained instructions on proper worship (2 Kings 22-23; 2 Chronicles 34). The king took great pain to follow every instruction of the Lord concerning proper worship.

Such examples as the cases of Hezekiah and Josiah clearly indicate the importance of presenting God with the proper worship He demands. Along with these are other instances of individuals who were condemned for inappropriate acts

Chapter Two

of worship. Cain's offering, which was a form of worship, was rejected (Genesis 4:3-5). Nadab's and Abihu's offering, an act of worship, was rejected (Leviticus 10:1-3). Perhaps most enduring in its negative impact was Jeroboam's introduction of corrupt worship (1 Kings 12; 1 Kings 14:16; 2 Kings 10:31; 2 Kings 13:6). If these records of Scripture teach us nothing else, they surely teach us that God has never taken worship lightly nor does He accept all forms of worship. His very nature demands unique worship. Anything less than this is unworthy of Him.

A cursory look at the Old Testament reveals that God is concerned for how He is worshiped, but are there any such concerns indicated in the New Testament? Of first note is that Jesus did speak of false worship (Matthew 15:9; Mark 7:7). Matthew and Mark captured Jesus speaking about false worship as He addressed the hypocrisy of the Jewish leaders and their religious traditions. John captured Jesus' discussion with the Samaritan woman (John 4:1-24). The matter of worship location was addressed, but more importantly, the proper manner of worship was stated by Jesus. In addition to these references, the Scriptures reveal a charge against Paul for teaching others an improper way of worship (Acts 18:13; 24:14).

However, we must conclude that the instructions in the New Testament for how to worship are rather sparse compared to what we find in the Old Testament. Although we can find references to acts of worship here and there, we cannot find the same detail we find in the Old Testament. We can gather some information from texts that bring up incidental statements about worship. For example, there are references to singing in a corporate assembly (Ephesians 5:15-21; Colossians 3:12-17). We can find instructions concerning proper worship in the context of issues in Corinth (1 Corinthians 12-14) and in Ephesus (1 Timothy 2:1-15). There are references to praying and teaching in a corporate assembly (1 Timothy 2:1-15). There are references for the day that the early Christians gathered for worship (Acts 20:7; 1 Corinthians 16:1-2). There are also references to Christians observing communion and preaching during their worship assembly (Acts 20:7). What we do not find in all this is the specific, detailed instruction as to how the early Christians went about their worship. So, how are we to go about worshiping God today?

We are on safe ground if we abide by some key principles. The first principle is to remember that any true worship of God must begin with a true heart. As Jesus indicated to the hypocritical Jewish leaders of His day, the proper ritual without the proper condition of the heart makes for empty worship (Matthew 15:9). It really does not matter what we do as an act of worship in our assemblies if we do not have the proper "why." If the act is not coming from the right motive, if the heart has no desire or intention to live a God-honoring life, then the worshiper is only wasting time. There is such a thing as false or vain worship, and we would do well to note that this starts with the condition of the heart.

The second principle to remember is that we cannot approach God with anything or in any way we wish. Jesus' statement about worshiping in spirit and in truth clearly says something about what we do and how we do it (John 4:23-24). When we conjoin this statement with the various examples of worship found in the Old Testament, we can conclude that God cannot be approached in any way we please. To worship in spirit is to worship with sincerity. To worship in truth is to worship in accordance to what the Lord has revealed. This must include what He has revealed about Himself—which would include His character and nature. As opposed to the highly sexualized practices of the Canaanites in the worship of their gods, the God of heaven is holy and pure. This says something about how we express ourselves in worship before Him and the acts that we perform. For example, common, sinfully suggestive actions in popular concerts and club acts cannot be mimicked in worshiping the holy God of heaven. This is not congruent with His nature. Nor should we seek to co-opt any popular worldly practice as a means of offering worship to the triune God.

Chapter Two

This is a critical point in the current seeker-pleasing environment in which the church lives today. It is one thing to try to accommodate various learning styles to communicate the gospel. It is quite another to cater to the felt-needs of the unchurched and the barely churched. There is a distinction to be maintained between evangelizing and worshiping. Although there is some bleed over, we need to remember that the purpose of worship is to give our God the praise and honor due Him. The church must regularly meet to give God worship, and having unbelievers in the audience can also be opportunities to win them to the Lord. However, these meetings are for worship and should be focused on this goal. Evangelistic, seeker-focus gatherings have a different primary objective. These can take advantage of various ways to attract the unchurched and barely churched that are not necessarily suitable for Christian worship. Of course, nothing is appropriate that dishonors the Lord. However, what may be used in such an evangelistic program may not be suitable for the time of corporate worship. Where hosting a Christian rap concert, having a theatrical presentation of a Bible story, or having live interviews of Christian testimonies may be a strategic way of getting the attention of the unsaved, these things are not fitting for a time for the church to offer worship to the Lord. They may be great marketing strategies for drawing attention to the things of God, but they are no substitute for Christians gathering together in a time of corporate worship.

A third principle is that of recognizing the value of a pattern for worship. This is to say that there is value in seeking to examine and emulate how the early Christians engaged in their worship of the Lord. There are some indicators and some examples of what was done then by God's approval. Again, there is a lack of specificity as compared to approved Old Testament worship. They were told such things as where to gather, what instruments to use, who was to perform what acts, and other church things. The New Testament does not provide such granularity for how the early Christians worshiped. We must also realize that there are some things from the first-century worship experience that cannot be replicated today. Some of these are cultural items that were not designed to be replicated in a different time and place. However, the broad strokes of their worship can be detected, and the attempt to practice these things is wise.

How are we to worship?

We are to worship with singing. Singing praises to the Lord can be done in many forms and can be expressed in various cultures. What may be a form of praise in an African village can be vastly different in an African American context. The same can be said of other racial and cultural contexts. However, singing is singing—no matter the tune or cadence.

We are to worship with prayers. We do have scriptural guidance for male-led prayers in the corporate assembly of the church (1 Timothy 2:1-15). However, prayer is something in which the entire assembly engages. There is great encouragement, comfort, and strength in engaging our spirits together in communication with the Lord. He sees every heart, and He uniquely ministers to every Christian's needs as we reach out to Him with our prayers.

We are to worship with giving. There is a powerful principle in the Scriptures concerning this. The principle can be found in God's instructions for observing the Feast of Tabernacles (Deuteronomy 16:13-17). It can also be found in David's seeking to build an altar to the Lord (2 Samuel 24:23-25). The example of the early Christians' giving is based in this same concept (1 Corinthians 16:1-2; 2 Corinthians 9:6-15). Giving a financial offering in worship is a test of our love, our faith, and our devotion.

We are to worship with instruction from God's Word. We have a reference to this act with regard to Paul's ministry (Acts 20:7). The "first day of the week" language is the same as used in another gathering of the church (1 Corinthians 16:2) as well as with other significant events in the pre-church establishment ministry of Jesus (Luke 24:1; John 20:1; 20:19). Instruction from God's Word is critical to the spiritual life and development of the local church. It is designed to help it develop into the full stature of Christ (Ephesians 4:11-16).

We should worship with commemorating the Lord's sacrificial and salvific work for us (Acts 20:7; 1 Corinthians 11:23-26). This is a time of reflection, celebration, and proclamation for the local church. It is a re-centering period in which we are refocused on who we are. It is a time to reflect on the covenant that we have with our Lord.

These acts of worship are each interlaced with the heart of genuine fellowship and oneness. The Scriptures are replete with warnings and instruction to mitigate fellowship-disturbing attitudes and actions (Matthew 5:23-24; 18:15-17; John 17:20-21; 1 Corinthians 11:17-34; Philippians 2:1-4; 4:1-3). To seek to worship in the presence of strife is as difficult as to seek to live in a home with unresolved arguments. Worship is designed to draw us nearer to the Lord and to each other.

Final Thoughts

A study of how to worship God can branch off into several disparate positions. These are the result of centuries of Christian debate over various elements of worship. The early years of this 21st century have seen the efforts of churches to avoid or to ignore historical debates over what makes for acceptable worship. Even though Christians must avoid mutual condemnation over questionable matters in this arena, we must also seek to worship the Lord properly. Worship is to be a top-down, not a bottom-up, action. This means that we must always seek God's directions as to how we are to come before Him. We must not be dogmatic about this matter, but nor do we want to be disrespectful to the Lord.

For Further Thought

1. Why is worship so vital in our lives?
2. What does Paul's statement about the Scriptures teach us (1 Timothy 3:15-17)?
3. What does the Old Testament teach us about worship?
4. What is the legitimacy of distinguishing between corporate worship and evangelism?
5. Why does the discussion of how to worship become so controversial?
6. How does culture impact how we worship?
7. Why are our local church relationships so important to our worship?
8. What are some things that you do to prepare yourself to worship?

Chapter Three

Studies in Worship
Cain & Abel

Introduction
Of all of the instances of worship found in the Scriptures, the episode of Cain and Abel seems to be the most enigmatic. Yet, their acts of worship serve as a powerful example of the connection of worship with daily life. This is particularly true in the matter of our horizontal relationships.

Characters in Contrast
After the devastating darkness brought upon human life because of sin, Adam and Eve began their lives in a now-fallen world. The original Eden experience was over. No longer did they have the free bounty of God's provisions as before. It would take intense, life-exhausting labor to have the ground produce its bounty (Genesis 3:17-19). It would take the experience of excruciating pain to perpetuate the human race (Genesis 3:16). A marital union once expressive of deeply cherished appreciation had been seeded with resentment and the resultant disharmony associated with bitterness (Genesis 2:21-25; 3:12). We can surmise that even humanity's existence with the animal creation suffered disturbance (Genesis 9:5-6). It was certainly a world far removed from God's creation intent. Into this world come Cain and Abel.

Cain is the firstborn of human procreation (Genesis 4:1). His name means "possession" or "possessed." He is described as a tiller of the ground. Cain's occupation is in line with man's newly defined role of working the earth to bring forth its yield. Cain's work is an honorable profession, so there is nothing to indicate that he was forcibly elected to be in a lower status before the Lord compared to that of Abel.

Abel was the second-born son (Genesis 4:2). There is no indication as to the time between the birth of these sons. We are simply told that Abel was born after Cain. It is interesting to note that his name means "vanity" or "nothingness." This could either be a reflection on the futility of human life or somewhat of a prophetic view toward the brevity of his life. Since we are given no indication of a prophetic revelation on Eve's part, the former is most likely. Abel's honorable occupation was caring for animals. Given that life in a post-Eden, fallen world would require agriculture, food sustenance, and clothing, both sons had chosen needed professions.

Offerings in Contrast

The Scriptures do not give us full detail of the offerings presented by the men, the amount of time that passed before they brought the offerings, or the instruction that they received to bring an offering. However, what is provided serves well for us as lessons for *how* to and *how not* to worship.

First, the concept of offering needs clarity. The Hebrew term *minchah*, used in a secular sense, was descriptive of humans presenting a gift of honor to a superior. This sense is further conveyed in the religious realm. God was to be honored by means of a physical offering. Therefore, the offerings presented by Cain and Abel centered in the thought of honoring the Lord God with a gift of tribute. In other words, these offerings were expressions of what each man thought about the Lord God.

This is a critical element in understanding what worship is. It is not a matter of pious acts performed as a duty. It is more of an opportunity to express the thoughts of our hearts toward God.

Chapter Three

This episode is not accompanied with details of God commanding an offering. We can deduce this conclusion, and we would be on safe ground in doing so, but there is also the possibility that the offerings were initiated by the men themselves. Regardless, the point to be made is that true worship emanates from the heart of the worshiper. We ought to want to honor the Lord. This needs to be a heartfelt desire. Short of this, we easily fall into merely going through religious acts (Matthew 15:9).

Cain's offering was a grain offering. Abel's offering consisted of animal portions. We are told that Cain's was rejected while Abel's was accepted. We are not given the specifics of why, but these can be easily deduced. Abel's offering was presented with careful forethought and a determination to present the best of what he had to the Lord (Genesis 4:4). He brought before the Lord the choicest of his flock and the best portions of the choicest animals ("their fat"). For Abel, nothing but the best should be offered before the Lord. He was committed to honoring the Lord God with the best. God looked at Abel's offering favorably. The Hebrew term shah conveys an intentional, scrutinizing look as opposed to a casual glance. The Lord carefully looked at Abel's offering. What was He examining? It was Abel's heart. This is a recurring theme throughout the Old Testament (Deuteronomy 6:4-5; 1 Samuel 13:14; 2 Kings 23:1-3; Jeremiah 17:10). The Lord saw the intent of the heart accompanied by the offering, and He approved.

Cain approached this offering with a different mindset. We must note that there was nothing about a grain offering that was somehow inferior. Scholarly debate continues over the nature of these offerings. Was Cain's rejected because he offered no blood sacrifice for atonement for sin? This is unlikely in that there is no evidence of atoning sacrifices being commanded at this time. These men simply presented offerings based on their individual occupations. Cain's problem was not in what he offered; it was in the heart behind the offering. The record reads that Cain brought an offering, but he did not bring the best offering he could have. God's gaze and inspection of Cain's offering revealed that Cain had not put his all into it. The inferiority was not in grain versus meat. It was in a lesser sense of honor, gratitude, and thanksgiving of heart. Cain's spirit was not right. God rejected the matter of the heart behind the act.

The tragic consequences of Cain's rejection was the murder of his own brother (Genesis 4:8). The Lord had warned Cain against the crouching, devouring, and dominating nature of his sin nature. He told Cain that this carnal natured required mastering (Genesis 4:7). Sadly, Cain chose to be mastered by it, and this choice cost Abel his life. The first sacrifice resulted in the first murder. It would take the ultimate sacrifice of the Christ to provide atonement for all sin.

Lessons for Worship

The tragic case of Cain and Abel provides powerful lessons for our worship today. First, we learn the importance of being intentional in our worship. Worship of the omnipotent, omniscient, and omni-present God of heaven and earth cannot be a last-minute and haphazard enterprise. It requires a mind that has a reverent approach to the Lord at the forefront. Moses could not approach the burning bush with common-worn sandals, and we cannot approach worship with casual thought. We must consider Whom we are approaching and our unworthiness to do so (Isaiah 6:5). We must reflect on all that He is and all that He does. We must be focused on His purity, righteousness, majesty, holiness, justice, and wholly-other nature. We must approach Him with a mind of reverence and a will of obedience. This was Abel's mindset toward his worship. Cain's approach to worship did not well up from these thoughts.

Second, we learn the value of planning for worship. Abel's intentionality of worship required careful planning. He, no doubt, had in mind how he was going to prepare his offering and what kind of animals he was going to use. While raising these animals, he surely had in his mind's eye the ones that he would sacrifice in this offering. So must it be with our total worship. Our giving in worship needs to be planned (1 Corinthians 16:1-2). The

Chapter Three

thoughts that we want to express in prayer need to be planned. When Jesus taught His disciples how to pray, He mentioned the petition for daily bread (Matthew 6:11). Paul wrote to the church instructions to pray for specific persons and officials (1 Timothy 2:1-4). These examples help us to see the value of preplanning for prayer. Our corporate time of prayer can be richly enhanced by the specificity of the requests being known ahead of time. It is also this way with other items of our corporate worship. Song directors and preachers should approach worship with a plan. To stand before an assembly with no prior thought of how to lead it in worship is irresponsible at best. Whether we are leading a particular element of worship or participating non-leading ways, our worship should be planned.

Third, we learn to worship with sincerity of heart. We cannot be unfair in evaluating Cain and say that he was insincere. However, we can look at Abel and see the beauty of his sincerity. Our planning for worship should never be reduced to form and function without thought to sincerity. Planning requires consideration for form and function if orderliness is to be expected and experienced (1 Corinthians 14:40). However, no plan for worship should become so rigid that it cannot make allowances for genuine expressions of sincerity. For example, a song can become so moving during the worship experience that it becomes prolonged or even repeated because of the impact that it is having on the assembly. The same can be said for a sermon being presented. The point to be made is that genuine expression is at the core of worship. Planning and order should help to enhance such expression—not to mute it. On the other hand, we must be careful not to confuse expressions of sincerity with expressions of personal vanity and aggrandizement.

Last, we learn to worship in faith. The beautiful testimony to Abel is that he worshiped in faith (Hebrews 11:4). We have to accept the fact that there is some mystery in attempting to understand what the Hebrew writer meant by declaring Abel's offering to be one done by faith. Admittedly, we are not given information in the Genesis account concerning God's commanding the men to provide an offering. Therefore, it is difficult to understand how Abel made his offering in a faith-response to a command of God. Such reasoning would indicate that Cain did not present his offering as a faith-response to God's instructions. However, we must clearly accept that what Abel did was motivated by his faith in the Lord. This can be inclusive of His belief in and beliefs about the God of heaven. Suffice it to say that while both brothers believed in God, Abel's belief incorporated a strong desire to please the Lord with an offering of his heart along with that of his sacrifice.

The Hebrew writer stated that faith in God includes the belief that He is a rewarder of those who earnestly seek after Him (Hebrews 11:6). This is surely what was in Abel's mind. Having never personally had union with the Lord like his parents, Abel had to have known of the Lord. He had to have known of His grace even in the face of banishment (Genesis 3:15). Abel wanted to please Him and was desirous of His favor. Thus, his offering was saturated in faith. When we desire union with God, and the mind is convinced of His glorious and gracious nature, the worship is heartily presented. Such a presentation was lacking in Cain's worship.

For Christians, worshiping by faith is reaching to follow God's worship directives, doing so with a desire to please Him, doing so with a longing to have union with Him, and doing so in recognition of His gracious favor.

Final Thoughts

Cain and Abel present us with the first cases on worshiping God. If we take away nothing else from their example, we need to take with us the vital importance of our motivation for worship. The pain of paradise lost by their parents should have made an indelible mark on their hearts. Such a tragic loss of that union, coupled with even vague and shadowy thoughts of redemption (Genesis 3:15), should have sparked the best from both of them.

Chapter Three

Sadly, only one saw worship in this way. Let us learn to pursue our worship with the mind of Abel, not Cain.

For Further Thought

1. How can we see Cain's attitude toward worship today?
2. What are some causes of a wrong attitude toward worship?
3. What are some practical ways of avoiding a wrong attitude toward worship?
4. How do we develop a grateful heart toward God?
5. What are some additional lessons from Abel's worship example?
6. Why is God so concerned for the worshiper's heart?
7. What is the connection between worship of God and having a relationship with God?
8. How can the local church best encourage the worship example demonstrated by Abel?

Drawing Nearer

Chapter Four

Studies in Worship
Abraham

Introduction
He is the father of the Israeli nation. He was the recipient of God's great redemptive, saving promise. He has gone down in history as the friend of God (James 2:23). He occupies a prominent place in both Old and New Testaments. He is revered for his faith in God. As such, Abraham serves as a tremendous example for us in learning how we are to worship the Lord of glory.

The Life and Times of Abraham
We are first introduced to him as a man of a pagan background (Joshua 24:2-4). His original name, Abram, means "exalted father." He is more famously known as Abraham, which means "father of a great multitude." Reading the accounts of Stephen and Moses, we learn that the Lord called Abram while he dwelt in Mesopotamia prior to his move to Haran (Acts 7:2-3). The family moved together from Ur (present-day Iraq) en route to Canaan, but they ended up in Haran (Genesis 11:27-32). Abram's father, Terah, died in Haran. After his father's death, Abram, Sarai (his wife), and Lot (his nephew) made their way into Canaan.

Abram showed himself as a man of faith and of worship. After arriving in Shechem, he built an altar to the Lord (Genesis 12:7).

Drawing Nearer

This was near an area known for remarkable oak trees or a quite notable tree (Moreh). He moved from Shechem near to Bethel, and there he built another altar and worshiped the Lord (Genesis 12:8). We are not given detailed information as to how Abram came to the decision to build altars to the Lord. The Hebrew term itself means "place of slaughter."

Although the Scriptures do not present information on the blood-sacrifice system at this point in the narrative, they do provide detailed information on this system later in the Pentateuch. It is reasonable to postulate that Abram's altar-building was done in response to his wanting to honor God. It is speculative to say with certainty that he was offering a blood sacrifice. However, it is clear that he was performing some sense of offering as an act of worship. Suggestions that Abram's altar-building was based in his pagan family background are speculative at best. We are on greater solid ground concluding that he was acting as a faith-response to the Lord who called him (Genesis 12:8).

Upon his return from Egypt, we find Abram again reaching out to the Lord at the altar he had built near Bethel (Genesis 13:4). In possession of much livestock, Abram's offering of blood sacrifices at this time is quite plausible.

The Lord spoke to Abram again after Abram and Lot had separated—Lot having moved to Sodom and Abram to the land of Canaan (Genesis 13:5-17). After this encounter, Abram moved to Hebron and again built an altar to the Lord (Genesis 13:18).

Undoubtedly, in the greatest faith-trial of his life, Abraham (Abram) was still a worshiping man. God had instructed him to sacrifice his son (Genesis 22:1-9). The birth and life and future of Isaac was the only physical, tangible evidence that Abraham had for God's fulfilling His promise to bless the world through Abraham's descendants. Still, Abraham was intent of performing God-honoring worship.

This brief sketch of Abram's life enables us to see that worship was a constant in his life. His example provides us with tremendous lessons for worship that we can apply individually and corporately.

Chapter Four

Lessons for Worship

Our first lesson from Abraham is to learn to worship the one true God. Coming from a pagan background, Abraham was not willing to continue in such bankrupt worship. His move from pagan worship to the worship of the God of heaven needs to be greatly admired. This is especially true when we consider that God had yet to form Israel and give them His commandment against idolatry (Exodus 20:1-6). It is also remarkable when we consider Abraham's period of neighboring with Canaanite (Genesis 12:6). Biblical historians have discovered the sordid and reprehensible details of the Canaanite religion—including sexual debauchery in the name of Baal (Baals as this was polytheistic religion) and Ashtoreth (also polytheistic) worship (Numbers 22:41; Hosea 2:13, 17; 1 Kings 11:5, 33; Judges 2:13). The Old Testament provides ample warning to God's people not to engage in such practices. Joshua called for Israel to rid themselves of Canaanite religion as the nation moved into its inheritance (Joshua 24:23). This would prove to be a snare to Israel throughout Old Testament history. However, from the beginning of his call, it was never a snare to Abraham.

We are living in the midst of a strong tide of rejection of the God of Scripture. Our time is one in which the Bible itself is being minimized in the minds of those caught up in humanistic, relativistic thinking and subjective truth. Masses are rejecting the very concept of divine authority while simultaneously accepting the authority of popular secular opinion. In such an environment, people are encouraged to place their faith in themselves and to reject objective truth and divine revelation. The world is creating gods of self and jettisoning the righteous ruler of all the earth. We are facing the daily challenge of confirming who has our loyalty. We must decide who shall receive our worship. This decision is not limited to a day of worship. It is inclusive of all of life. As our Lord Jesus showed, that loyalty cannot be divided (Matthew 4:10). Abraham chose to worship the Lord. What choice will we make?

Drawing Nearer

A second lesson we learn from Abraham is the need to worship wherever we are. Abraham's somewhat nomadic existence did not get in the way of his need for worship. Wherever he traveled, he built an altar. He needed to keep the presence of God ever near him. He wanted to ensure the steadfastness of his faith. He desired to stay focused on God's promise. He was intent on keeping life in proper perspective no matter where he would be led. In this way, he shows us the absolute necessity of worship in our lives.

Our God cannot be limited to a particular place and time, and neither should our faith be limited to familiar geographical constraints. For some, God is God so long as they are in places and around people expecting them to worship the Lord. This has been the experience of some college students. They are there to worship the Lord in weekly services and be mindful of their living while among family and local church members. However, once freed from such an environment, accountability is lost, and their faith-walk is buried in the presence of those who do not honor Him. This isn't just an issue for some younger people either. Christians of every age range somehow find it easy to leave the Lord at home. He does not accompany them on the job, at the store, out to dinner, at entertainment venues, or on vacations. For too many Christians, the worship of God is a Sunday thing that never crosses the borders of other territories of life experiences.

When we keep in mind that worship is a daily experience as well as a corporate experience, we will build an altar everywhere we go. Those around us will know who we are and what we stand for. They will recognize us as a worshiping person, and this will give us a witness that cannot be ignored. It will not be that we speak so much as that we behave in a way that witnesses our dedication to the Lord. We do not have to be in the corporate assembly to be in the presence of God. Our lives are to be an act of worship and an erected altar no matter where we are.

Abraham's worship life offers a third significant lesson. It is that we must worship even when afflicted by life crisis. In his initial steps in his faith walk with the Lord, Abram entered into

Chapter Four

foreign territory (Genesis 12:10—13:4). This was a terrifying episode for Abram. He was already facing the fear of famine, which is why he moved down to Egypt. He was facing the very real threat of losing his life. This fear moved him to deceive the Egyptians into thinking that Sarai was his sister and not his wife. We must remember that this is the same man who had built altars and called on the Lord near the Oak of Moreh and near Bethel. However, he had a life crisis in Egypt, and fear moved him to operate in his power as opposed to operating by God's promise. The Lord's providence turned this situation into victory for Abram and Sarai. Not only was Abram's life spared and Sarai's honor maintained, but they also left Egypt quite wealthy. Having left Egypt, Abram again worshiped the Lord (Genesis 13:4).

Times of life crisis are especially times in which to honor God with our worship. Abram's time of crisis proves that this is easier said than done. We often react as he did when the dark clouds enter our lives. We can experience significant periods of time in which God's favor is clearly evident in our lives. These are periods in which our worship is filled with praise for all that God has done and is doing in our lives. However, such deep-welled and euphoric praise can become blunted over times of prolonged tangible favor. This life is not designed to be lived without times of trial (James 1:1-12). It is in such times of trial that we must learn to still praise the Lord with our worship. The life crisis is an opportunity to cry out to the Lord, draw nearer to Him, lean heavily upon him, and give great praise to Him— even while we are in the storm. Again, this is not easy to do nor is it deemed realistic by worldly standards. Yet—this is what we are called to develop in life.

In his later years, Abraham had developed this mindset (Genesis 22:1-9). When God tested him with another life crisis, this one concerning the very heart of God's promise to him, Abraham did not hesitate to go forward. He did not devise another plan. He had no question about God's direction. He was steadfast in offering God worship—even at the expense of his son, Isaac's life. He was going to offer this worship to the

Lord with full confidence in God's mighty deliverance (Genesis 22:5; Hebrews 11:17-19). As we continue our Christian journey, we are being led into a spiritual maturity that will enable us to give the Lord genuine worship even in time of crisis. The worship in the times of crisis draws us to even greater heights and deeper depths of praising and honoring our God with all that is within us.

Abraham's experience offers a fourth lesson concerning worship. We must worship the Lord even in times of delayed blessing. Abram's initial trek began with a promise of great blessing. This "exalted father" had no physical evidence of God's promise coming to fruition. He was already advanced in years (75 years old) when he set out from Haran. Yet, he continued to offer God worship even as he endured a 25-year journey of faith in God's promise. This journey took him through the Egyptian crisis (Genesis 13), the deliverance of his nephew (Genesis 14), the actual covenant-making experience (Genesis 15), the imbroglio of Hagar and Ishmael (Genesis 16), the trial with Abimelech (Genesis 20), and finally the initial fulfillment of the promise with the birth of Isaac (Genesis 21). All this led Abraham to the pinnacle of trial in the commanded offering of Isaac (Genesis 22). Throughout it all, Abraham remained a man of worship.

The Christian life is one of worship. From the time when we come to know the Lord until the time we are called from this life, we are to be people who worship the Lord. Over this time, we may find ourselves longing for the Lord to bless our lives and show His favor in some critical areas of life. These things may be very near and dear to us. They may even be considered life-sustaining to us. Our Lord has promised to grant us all that we need in this life. Yet, we may have periods in life where such provisions, persons, or benefits are not soon granted. Still, we must honor the Lord with our worship. Even when it seems as if we have been somehow overlooked by heaven while being cursed on earth, the Lord deserves our worship. A promise seemingly delayed is not a promise reneged.

Chapter Four

Final Thoughts

Abraham's life offers us a wealth of lessons concerning worship. His experiences help us to step back and see the moments of our own lives that need to feed into a deeper worship experience. When we are able to see the whole of our lives thus far from the prospective of God's providence, our mindset for worship will reflect the kind of reverence that our Lord is due.

For Further Thought

1. What are some current-day challenges we face regarding worshiping the true God?
2. Why do some people limit their worship to a church assembly?
3. What is the connection between worshiping God and walking by faith?
4. Why do times of crisis cause us to lose focus on worship?
5. How do times of crisis help us to develop deeper times of worship?
6. Why must worship be a lifelong experience?
7. How do our life experiences enhance our worship?
8. What are some additional lessons on worship from Abraham's life?

Drawing Nearer

Chapter Five

Studies in Worship
Jacob

Introduction
The story of Jacob serves as a clear example of the God-breathed Scriptures. This is because Jacob comes across as somewhat of an anti-hero. His character, warts and all, is laid bare for us to see. A mere human biographer would have likely spared us of the negatives and exaggerated the positives. Yet, as it stands, Jacob's life gives us much to consider as we further examine our worship of God.

From Heel-Grabber to Humbled Worshiper
Perhaps the story of Esau's and Jacob's birth is among the most noteworthy captures of the Old Testament record. They were born twins, but the indication is that they did not favor each other. Esau was distinguished by his reddish, hairy look (Genesis 25:24-25). We are later told that Jacob was smooth-skinned.

The most significant note about the boys' birth is the prophecy concerning them (Genesis 25:23). Esau's offspring were to be inferior to Jacob's. Rachel's pregnancy was a difficult one. Jacob, the second out of the womb, came out holding his brother's heel. This was a foreshadow of the major life-changing events that lay ahead of the family. It was also predictive of the subordinate position of Jacob's progeny over that of Esau's. The curious nature of Paul's statement concerning the two boys should be understood in relation to God's favoring of Jacob over Esau (Romans 9:10-13). Such favor was a function of God's foreknowledge of their self-determined paths in life.

Esau grew up to be a skillful hunter (Genesis 25:27). This was much to the liking of his father. On the other hand, Jacob tended to be more of a homebody and probably what some might described as a "momma's boy" (Genesis 25:27-28). One can almost picture the tension of this household. It is a tension that would play out poorly for all concerned.

One day, Esau came in from hunting and was in a rage of hunger. He found Jacob having prepared food, and he bargained with Jacob to be fed (Genesis 25:29-34). The bargain was over Esau's birthright. The birthright tradition gave the firstborn son headship over the clan (in the patriarchal system) and a double portion of his father's estate. Additionally, in the patriarchal system, the birthright included the promises of God for a divinely blessed and prosperous future (Genesis 27:4, 27-29). Biblical archaeologists have discovered evidence of legal exceptions to birthright privileges being granted to the firstborn son.

We are told that Esau despised his birthright (Genesis 25:34), which means that he viewed it disdainfully. He was so fixed on his current condition that he thought nothing of this cherished blessing. Only when he lost it did he come to a sense of volcanic anger and inconsolable regret (Hebrews 12:16-17).

In time, Isaac came to the point of death. His sight had seriously deteriorated. He called for Esau to confer to him the birthright, and he was doubtless unaware of the previous bargain exchange between his two sons. Esau carried no sense of this exchange either. Jacob must have told Rebekah of the bargain he had made with Esau. She devised a plan of deception that resulted in Isaac's granting the birthright to Jacob instead of Esau (Genesis 27:1-40). From that point forward, Esau looked for an opportunity to kill Jacob. It was Rebekah's further intervention that caused Jacob's life to be spared. She had Jacob sent away his home to the

Chapter Five

land of Padan Aram—the home of her brother, Laban (Genesis 27:41—28:5). Jacob's journey involved an amazing dream that would both startle and bless his life. It is from this point in his life that Jacob's life provides us with critical lessons on worship.

Lessons for Worship

Though headed to a certain destination, Jacob's fleeing of Esau initially found him in the direction of Haran. This was the city where Terah, Abram's father had died (Genesis 11:31) and from which Abram had set out to the land of Canaan. For Jacob, it became a God-recognizing and God-encountering experience (Genesis 28:10-22).

Jacob's immediate reaction to his dream was to recognize that the Lord had encountered him (Genesis 28:16). The Lord met Jacob where the man was. He met Jacob as a frightened and conniving man running for his life. We can safely assume that Isaac had instructed Jacob concerning the God of his father and of himself. We can surmise that Jacob's life prior to His encounter with God was lived without great regard for divine ethics. Neither he nor Rebekah had behaved honorably in their deception of Isaac.

Among the greatest lessons for worship gleaned from Jacob is our need for recognizing and encountering God (Genesis 28:16). It is the realization that we have come into the presence of the Sovereign, Holy, and wholly-other One. This speaks to both the reverential and the relational aspect of Christianity. The former exhorts us to always realize who we are coming before, and the latter reminds us that we are called to be in union with Him. Christianity is not some cold, sterile religion. Rather, it is a relational way of life driven by the recognition that God has called us to Himself. No Christian should ever engage in worship for mere ceremony. God is much too awesome in every way for us not to see our opportunities for worship as opportunities for a genuine divine encounter with the Sovereign Lord of all.

A second lesson from Jacob's life is found in the conditions that led to his initial encounter with the Lord. We are told that

Drawing Nearer

Jacob was a homebody, content to stay around his mother. There are no particular indications of his being attuned to the things of God. Yet, in his time of crisis, he was ripe for an encounter with the Lord.

There are times in which God has to shake our world to gain our attention. Modern history has shown how quickly people come to prayer in times of national crisis. National and international duress drive us to prayer. Mass shootings and other such tragedies push us into houses of worship. Personal bouts of deadly diseases force us to look for divine intervention. Clearly, God has a way of shaking us up. In such times, our world is reduced to the simple reality of what life in this world is all about (Ecclesiastes 12:13-14). These are God-recognizing and God-encountering moments in which we learn to look to Him as our only hope. We are wise to have this thought in mind as a matter of course as opposed to God having to get our attention. Our regular worship should be our refocus period that keeps us from God needing to get our attention.

Jacob's life brings to us a third strong lesson. It is the connection between worship and recommitment. When morning had come, Jacob set up a memorial stone and consecrated it. Oil was an important substance to carry on journeys. It could be used for food and for bodily care. His recognition of his encounter with the Lord was much too important for him to forget where it occurred. Calling this place Bethel (House of God) is a further indication of the impact his encounter with God had on him. Jacob made a vow of dedication to the Lord and sought His favor for the journey ahead.

Among other things, our corporate worship must be a time of recommitment. It is an opportunity for us to recognize, reflect, and reconfirm. *Recognition* speaks to whom we are giving our obeisance. *Reflection* speaks to consideration of God's favor toward us in the past week. *Reconfirming* speaks to our determination to live a life for Him in the days to come. One might read Jacob's words as somewhat of a bargaining with God (Genesis 28:20-22). Such thoughts may have been in Jacob's heart. However, our recommitting ourselves is not a matter of bargaining with God. It is not a matter of saying, "Lord, if You are good to me, then I will live right before You." Rather, it is a determined spirit that declares to put forth every effort to live a God-honoring life in recognition of and reflection on who He is—regardless of how well things are going for us. When we can get to the place of disassociating thoughts of proper living and good deeds from being recipients of God's blessings, we will have in mind what the Lord desires of us. This can be difficult, because the Scriptures teach much of the reaping and sowing principle. It is true that God grants favor to the obedient. It is true that we reap what we sow. However, it is equally true that God does not owe us anything good. If we were to receive what we truly deserve from Him, it would not be a good thing (Romans 3:23; 6:23). Thankfully, He has not dealt with us in accordance with our sin (Psalm 103:10). Therefore, our worship is not a time of bargaining for favor. Rather, it is a time of saying we will live for Him whether He grants our earthly desires or not. Faith will move us to live for Him regardless (Daniel 3:16-18).

Another powerfully poignant lesson from Jacob concerning worship is the impact that our worship has on our lives. When Jacob fled from Esau, he experienced a powerful encounter with God. Having left from that experience, Jacob moved on to his encounter with his uncle, Laban, who turned out to be as deceptive in his dealings as Jacob had been with Esau and Isaac (Genesis 29:1—31:55). Jacob was tricked into marrying Leah and manipulated into seven more years of labor to be able to marry Rachel. Life with Laban and Jacob was a constant battle of trickery. The major elements of their relationship as reported in the Scriptures give us an indication of how their normal relationship must have functioned. In the end, the two titans of deception entered into a covenant to stay separated from each other and that Jacob would do right by Laban's daughters (Genesis 31:43-55).

Any true worshiper of God must ask himself what impact worship has made upon his life. Has she had a change of behavior with regard to her home life? Has his demeanor on the job changed for the better? Is God being honored or embarrassed by their behavior in and among the community of faith? These are not questions to be easily dismissed. We simply cannot afford to allow worship to be disconnected from our lives in this world. Many Christians compartmentalize their lives. Their identity in the corporate worship is separate and apart from their identity elsewhere. However, we must be diligent to maintain a consistency of who we are wherever we are. Our environment can and will change, but our core must remain the same. The popular saying, "What would Jesus do" became just another trite cliché to many. What really matters is how conscious I am of my thoughts and behavior wherever I am. Let us avoid the need to erect a pillar of rocks based on ungodly behavior between us and others. God is witness to our thoughts, words, and deeds in worship, work, home, and even while alone.

Jacob's return to his homeland provides another poignant worship lesson for us. In his trepidation in meeting Esau, Jacob sought the Lord for protection and favor (Genesis 32:9-12). It was at the foot of the Promised Land that Jacob had another Divine-human experience that impacts our thoughts on worship (Genesis 32:22-32). We learn that worship often involves a wrestling with God. Though scholarly debate exists over whether this was a physical encounter with an angel or more of a dreamlike, mental period of anguish, the lesson to be learned remains regardless.

In contemporary times, the popular picture of worship is that of a celebrative, enthusiastic, and even concert-like, euphoric experience. What is often missed is the angst of worship. Angst is not caused by questions of God's existence. Rather, it is caused by concerns over God's care for us. Does He know what I am dealing with? Does He care enough about this to act beneficently on my behalf? Is He not granting new favor because of my past but repented-from sins? Is He holding my imperfection against me? Unfortunately, in contemporary worship approaches to create a worship experience more fitting to the perceived needs of the unchurched, we are missing our need as believers to wrestle

Chapter Five

with our personal struggles along the Christian journey. We forget that the path to final glory is laced with faith-poisoning trials (Acts 14:22). These are times when singing Christian "pop music" fails to get to the heart of what is on our hearts. These are moments when our inward man does not want to say words that we are really having problems singing. Worshiping in the midst of such life-drama forces us to wrestle with God.

The wrestling is a test of the tenacity of our faith. We are forced to answer by our actions whether it is worth holding on to Him when we feel He is not holding on to us. Like Jacob, we may leave the assembly or the private worship room having a limp. However, we will be the better for it. The child of God who worships the Lord and does not shy away from the wrestling match is the one whose worship elevates to a higher plain.

A final worship lesson from the life of Jacob comes to us from the last two major periods of his life. Here, we find him being called by the Lord back to Bethel (Genesis 35:1-7) and reuniting with Joseph in Egypt (Genesis 46:1—47:31). These two epochs of his life were more drama-filled than the prior periods.

Jacob had made a vow to the Lord during his initial flight from Esau (Genesis 28:10-22). When the Lord called him back to Bethel, 10 long, hard years had passed. Jacob had been living in Shechem. God had already told him to go back to his home area, but Jacob had delayed (Genesis 31:1-3). He had conditioned his allegiance to the Lord upon his safe return home, yet Jacob had not fulfilled his vow.

Whether we be engaged in corporate or private worship, it is a time of fulfilling our vow to the Lord. In one sense, this vow was made when we were baptized into Christ. Baptism is a pledge to death, a pledge for life, and a covenant commitment to the Lord (1 Peter 3:20-21). We voluntarily come under the Lordship of Jesus. We become His even while living in this world (1 Corinthians 6:19-20). Invariably, as we live day-to-day, we have moments of lapse in this spiritual reality. Thoughts are harbored, words are said, and deeds are done that do not reflect a person belonging to Jesus. It is in worship that we have an opportunity to reaffirm this ownership and reconsecrate ourselves. Jacob had to be called to do what he had promised. We should not need additional calls from heaven to do what we already promised to do on earth.

It is noteworthy that Jacob had his clan put away the idols that were among them (Genesis 35:2-4). Doubtless, this is something that he tolerated among them during and after his time with Laban. However, he knew that to come before the God of glory, such things had to be put away from his household. We can be tempted to avoid worship when we are conscious of sin in our lives. For some, the thought is to "perfect themselves" before coming to worship. The problem with such thinking is that it operates from thoughts of human ability to meet divine standards. Though it is commendable not to want to approach the Lord because we are aware of our imperfections, God's gracious invitation allows us to approach Him through Jesus in spite of our imperfections (Hebrews 4:14-16). Conversely, Jacob's actions teach us that we should never approach the Lord irreverently. Although we cannot perfect ourselves as a prerequisite of worship, we cannot ignore the need to have a contrite heart over the sin in our lives (Luke 18:9-14; 1 John 1:8-10).

Finally, at the end of his days, Jacob was found to be worshiping the Lord while leaning on his staff. A man who had seen many years of trial, some of which he brought upon himself, was now ready to die (Hebrews 11:21). His faith in the Lord was settled and secure. A lifetime of drama ended in a period of peace.

Our worship of the Lord is a sustaining force throughout our lives. The various trials that we face and the multitude of experiences that we have serve to feed into our worship experience. We leave worship only to encounter satanic attack, and this leads us back into worship. At the end of our days, may the Lord see us giving Him praise and thanksgiving while leaning on His everlasting arms.

Chapter Five

Final Thoughts

The way in which we start out in life does not determine how we will end up. The decisions we make along that way design our end state. Living our lives with a constant, recurring focus on worship, regardless of the wrong turns we have made, will navigate us to a blessed end.

For Further Thought

1. What are some critical lessons to be learned from Isaac and Rebekah concerning their children?
2. What does Jacob's early life reveal about his thoughts toward God?
3. How did Jacob's initial vision experience impact his life?
4. How did God initially get your attention?
5. What has been the impact of God's initial calling upon your life?
6. What are some reasons that Christians shy away from worship?
7. What is the value of considering a vow in conjunction with worship?
8. How does our worship life impact our final state in this world?

Drawing Nearer

Chapter Six
Studies in Worship
Nadab & Abihu

Introduction
Nadab and Abihu are well-known characters among Bible students. They are also among the most notorious outlaws of Old Testament history. Their story is a cautionary tale of how not to approach the Lord. It is through them that we learn significant things about the Lord as well as discover some things about ourselves.

A Tale of Two Young Men
The book of Leviticus covers two crucial aspects of being in a covenant relationship with God: how to approach the Lord and how to fellowship (commune) with the Lord. The case of Nadab and Abihu teaches us about our approach to Him.

The descendants of Abraham had been through destiny-shaping experiences. For 400 long years, they were enslaved by the Egyptians. God raised up Moses to deliver them from the Egyptians. He delivered a death blow to that nation and forced its king to recognize that God is God. By the time of Nadab and Abihu, Israel had been delivered from bondage and had been formed as a special people of God. The Lord had given them

Drawing Nearer

His commandments. In the case of Nadab and Abihu, He vividly demonstrated what it means to be in covenant relationship with a holy God.

The two men were Aaron's oldest sons (Exodus 6:23). As such, they were granted the privilege of working in a priestly role (Exodus 28:1). Prior to this, they were among the select few to come nearer to God on Mount Sinai (Exodus 24:1-9). This brief scriptural mention of Nadab and Abihu initially paints a good picture. We can imagine Aaron's and even Moses' pride in having their sons/nephews being blessed to take part in God's service in a special way. Sadly, the picture quickly turned dark.

In the midst of making a series of offerings before the Lord, a tragic episode took place. Moses had been leading Israel in these acts of worship as God had instructed him (Leviticus 1:1—7:38). He was then commanded to consecrate Aaron and his sons for their priestly duties (Leviticus 8:1—9:24). We repeatedly read of how they meticulously followed God's commands.

After these things, Nadab and Abihu are pointed out as acting outside of God's commandment (Leviticus 10:1-3). Having gone through an elaborate seven-day ceremony in which they were purified and dedicated for the priestly office, they quickly profaned it. They did so in offering "strange fire" before the Lord. This resulted in their immediate deaths.

What is meant by "strange fire" has been and remains a subject of debate and speculation. A kaleidoscope of explanations have been given as to why judgment came upon Nadab and Abihu. One explanation is that their sin was taking the fire from the wrong location (they used an incense offering). According to this view, they used an unholy source of fire—one that God had not kindled—and sought to make an offering with it. The Scriptures do teach us that God sent down fire on an occasion in connection with an offering (2 Chronicles 7:1). However, the altar fire at the occasion of Nadab's and Abihu's judgment seems to have already been kindled by natural means. Sacrifices had already been offered by a previously kindled fire (Leviticus 9:6-13). We can therefore understand the miraculous manifestation

Chapter Six

at the sacrifice prior to Nadab's and Abihu's sinful actions to be a miracle of consuming the sacrifices as opposed to a miracle of a special fire (Leviticus 9:24). Therefore, taking fire from a human-generated source as opposed to a divine one does not seem to have been their sin.

Another explanation is that Nadab and Abihu were condemned for making their offering at the wrong time. This explanation is based largely on God's commands to Moses after the young priest's death (Leviticus 16:1-2). Aaron was given specific instructions not to enter into the Holy Place within the tabernacle at will. As High Priest, he was allowed entrance once a year on the Day of Atonement. Using this backdrop, the argument is made that Nadab and Abihu sought to enter into the Holy Place and were summarily executed.

Although this is a plausible explanation, it does appear to be reading the narrative backwards. We would have to assume that the instructions concerning when to enter the Holy Place had been given prior to what we read in the narrative.

A third explanation concerning the young priests' demise is that they were condemned for being intoxicated. This explanation centers on the prohibition given shortly after God's judgment upon them (Leviticus 10:8-10). Again, the weakness of this explanation lies in the narrative's order. The assumption would have to be made that the prohibition had previously been known and then purposefully violated.

Given the forgoing, we are still faced with the question as to what was Nadab's and Abihu's sin. We are safe to conclude that it was the spirit behind each of the offered explanations. Their act was arrogantly presumptuous. The Scriptures reveal that they did what God had not authorized. The "strange" fire was something unauthorized, something of non-relatedness or non-acquaintance with the Lord and His will. The spirit of the narrative indicates that they knew better than to do this, but they did so regardless. It takes a high-minded person to act in this way. The action was tantamount to disregarding God's wholly-other nature and treating Him as common.

Lessons for Worship

The tragic story of Nadab and Abihu still serves as a strong cautionary tale for Christians today. There is much for us to consider both in terms of how we are to approach the Lord and how we must carefully apply this narrative. We begin with the latter.

One of the dangers of seeking application of this event is making it say much more than it was ever intended to communicate. This is a particular danger in seeking to apply Nadab's and Abihu's case to modern-day worship. These young priests' actions have historically been used as a caution against popular controversies in Christian worship. Perhaps most popular is the use of this narrative to condemn instrumental music in worship. This involves an argument of inclusion and exclusion. In short, the logic is that when the Lord commands something in particular, then this automatically condemns anything else. For example, when God told Noah to use gopher wood in the building of the ark, He excluded any other kind of wood. The conclusion is that God had told these young priests what kind of fire to use, and they were condemned for using another kind of fire.

The challenge of such argumentation is in making the leap from offering strange fire to that of using instrumental music in worship. Admittedly, the evidence in the New Testament shows Christians worshiping without the aid of mechanical instruments of music. As previously mentioned, this is good reason for restorationist-minded Christians to avoid practices for which there is no New Testament precedent. However, we must not miss the greater application of this narrative. It is a tremendous lesson concerning the spirit behind our acts of worship. If we merely focus our efforts on making a direct connection to the use of instrumental music in worship, we will miss the core message of the text. Also, if we are not careful, the narrative can quickly be used as a referendum on proper worship attire, appropriate singing styles, or even church meeting times. The fact of the matter is that this narrative speaks to us much more about our spirit toward worship.

Chapter Six

Whenever we worship, privately or corporately, we must beware of having a wrong spirit. Worshipers of God must be as careful about the spirit behind our worship as we are with what actions we do in the worship. When it comes to our worship, the Lord is as concerned with the "why" of the worship as He is the "what" of the worship.

The critical lesson of this narrative is found in Moses' words to Aaron (Leviticus 10:3). The scene of the text is solemn and doubtless surreal. Aaron has witnessed his sons being consumed by fire. Their death was instantaneous. One can imagine their screams of anguish and the utter horror of all who witnessed their demise. Moses himself must have been shocked by this calamity. What a tragic scene this must have been! Yet, in the midst of the outbreak of this consuming fire, Moses had the presence of mind to speak God's solemn warning. Aaron, despite overwhelming sense of loss, held his peace. No one, regardless of who he or she may be, can approach the Lord as common.

If we must know anything about God, it must be the fact that He is holy. He is wholly other. He cannot be equated with anyone or anything. He is the source of all life and of all being. The opening words of the Holy Scriptures say it all (Genesis 1:1). At the start of our consciousness of being, there is God. It is not that He comes into being by our recognition. It is that we wake up and recognize His being. Our very existence is in His hands (Acts 17:28). This amazing world, still beyond the comprehension of the human mind, is His handiwork. The vast universe of the human body exemplifies just a modicum of His matchless creative power. He determines what nation of people will live where and how far, how long they will exist in a given region (Acts 17:26). He can never be sourced in anything, because He is the source of everything (Acts 17:24-25). There is no one like Him. This is the message delivered to Israel from the beginning (Exodus 20:1-7). It is the message that must remain in our minds and permeate our consciousness every single day. Therefore, worship begins with the recognition that God is, that He is holy, that He is wholly other, that He must be set apart from all else, and that He must be shown reverence. Any worship that does not start at this point is vain, futile, empty, worthless, and rejected worship. Somehow, Nadab and Abihu failed at this very point, and it cost them their lives.

How might people today fall under the same condemnation? One of the dangers in today's popular Christian world is the mindset to coming to God in worship. We have popularized a vision of God as our loving Father, as well we should. The Scriptures teach us to have the mindset of "Abba Father" (Romans 8:15). However, we must always lace this concept with the level of reverence due Him. God is not our "buddy." We are not on equal footing with Him. There must always be the clear recognition of the amazing magnitude of being graciously admitted into His presence at any time we desire (Hebrews 4:14-16). Though He calls us to come to Him as loving children, the fact is this: We are still the children.

Such recognition in our worship is paramount. It does have application to how we approach Him in personal worship. Our prayers, our reading of the Scriptures, our songs, and all other things that we do in our time of private worship must always be motivated and informed by our acknowledgment of who He is. The same applies to our corporate worship. Who He is demands that we approach His worship with deliberate purpose. Our worship mindset cannot be that of the casual attending of a sporting event or a fun social gathering. We are not coming to play cards with a friend. We are coming to worship the wholly other. The sandals must come off our feet because we are coming to stand on holy ground. This is something that Nadab and Abihu did not recognize, chose not to recognize, or became so "familiar" with God that they did not think they had to recognize.

It is worth mentioning again the danger of becoming legalistic with how we show our reverence in worship. For example, although this does say something about our attire, it does not demand formal dress. If it did, then we would have to consider matters of racial, cultural, and geographical norms. A financial, social-economic dimension would also need to be considered.

Chapter Six

The point is not about what one wears. Rather, it is the attire of one's heart. Legalism can also devolve into debates of what we do in our worship. This is more of an issue with our times of corporate worship. Though no God-fearing person believes that God's worship can include any act we wish, no one can dismiss the need for a reverential spirit to accompany the actions that we do perform. Individual congregations need to exercise wisdom in seeking scriptural direction for what they do in their worship. Anything done must have at its core the need to honor and revere the Lord for whom He has revealed Himself to be.

Finally, we must keep ourselves from a presumptuous spirit regarding our worship. We do not read of anything said by Nadab and Abihu in this tragic event. We can only speculate as to what they had said to anyone before acting without divine sanction. The fact that God had not commanded what they had done should not be missed or minimized. They were certainly instructed at some time and in some way counter to what they sought to do. They acted in arrogance. By doing anything that God had not commanded them, they were in effect taking God's prerogative. Their insolence had to be dealt with, and the Lord did not hesitate to do so.

For us to come before the Lord without regard for the condition of our hearts and the need to seek His directions for our worship is to act just as presumptuously. Even though we have not been given the same level of detail for our worship as Israel, we still must be careful in what we do. Sadly, those who are eager to deconstruct past traditions often offer no better path forward. If we are going to tear down a barn, it makes sense to first consider its replacement. Revolution can lead to an anarchy that even consumes the revolutionists. Human traditions regarding worship can and should change. However, those leading the charge for change need to carefully examine their hearts as to the true motivation for change.

Final Thoughts

Being holy means being set apart from all else. Our God must be revered, honored, and treated with the utmost degree of respect. He must remain set apart in our hearts. If the office of President of the United States is to be respected, God is to be respected more. If the judges and law enforcement agencies are to be respected, God is to be respected more. If doctors, teachers, parents, and preachers are to be respected, God is to be respected more. Nadab and Abihu somehow lost this sense of reverence. Let us not do the same.

For Further Thought

1. What are some examples of acting presumptuously?
2. What moves someone to act presumptuously before the Lord?
3. How does Israel's worship differ from Christian worship?
4. Why is it more challenging for us to know what things we should do in worship?
5. How does personal, private worship contribute to our corporate worship?
6. What are some of the dangers of changing our corporate worship traditions?
7. What are the positives and negatives of contemporary worship practices?
8. How do we best determine what we should and should not do in worship?

Chapter Seven
Studies in Worship
Saul of Kish

Introduction
The man who would become Israel's first king provides us another key insight about our worship. He was a head taller than all others who were considered as potential kings for the people. Sadly, his example is not one that we can esteem.

The Man Who Would Be King
A rags-to-riches story tends to catch our interest. The case with Saul of Kish is no exception. His story is set against the backdrop of difficult times for Israel. Samuel, the last judge, was God's guiding force for the people. He had been under the tutelage of Eli—the priest whose household was severely judged and condemned for failure to honor the Lord (1 Samuel 1:1—4:18). Now in his later years and having reared sons whose behavior was eerily similar to those of Eli, Israel pressed upon Samuel to have a king rule over the nation (1 Samuel 8:1-5). Samuel had bristled at the demand, so the Lord had to command him to acquiesce to the people. However, he forewarned them of the consequences of this action (1 Samuel 8:6-22). Saul would turn out to be that king.

Drawing Nearer

Though considered quite statuesque, Saul's confidence did not match his physique (1 Samuel 9:1-2). He lacked the warrior spirit of his father, Kish. He questioned Samuel's initial statement of his coming prominence (1 Samuel 9:19-21). He lacked the confidence to tell his uncle about his prophetic experience with Samuel (1 Samuel 10:16). He even hid himself from view when he was announced as Israel's new king (1 Samuel 10:17-27). Nevertheless, Saul was chosen by the Lord to be king over Israel, and he was prepared by the Lord to carry out this duty. The Lord made him a "new man" (1 Samuel 10:6) and promised to be with him (1 Samuel 10:7). Saul was instructed to wait in Gilgal for Samuel to come and perform his priestly duties (1 Samuel 10:8).

Samuel's instructions to Saul concerning Gilgal have been understood in different ways among linguistic scholars. At the core of the various interpretations is attempting to decipher when Saul was to go to Gilgal and whether two instances of going to Gilgal are in view. Was Samuel instructing Saul to go directly to Gilgal after their initial meeting (1 Samuel 10:1-8)? Was Samuel telling Saul that he should wait for him whenever Saul was to go to Gilgal? Were there two distinct instances of Saul traveling to Gilgal? The Hebrew terms used, and their grammatical construction, allow for some ambiguity. However, further reading of the narrative more likely indicates that Saul was not instructed to go directly to Gilgal. Rather, he was instructed to go there after the public declaration and recognition of him as king over the people. Once this was done, Saul returned to his home.

Though Saul had been announced as Israel's divinely chosen king, he lacked the full acceptance of the people. It would take his divinely enabled action of delivering the people in a time of crisis to convince the nation that God had chosen him as king. Saul led Israel in overturning an Ammonite attack, and this secured his rule (1 Samuel 11:1-14). At this juncture, Samuel led the nation to Gilgal for a renewal and heartfelt acceptance of Saul's kingship.

Gilgal had already been recognized as a special place during Joshua's time of leading the nation (Joshua 5:1-12). It served as

Chapter Seven

Israel's camp as the nation began to lay claim to the Promised Land. The Septuagint text (the Greek translation of the Old Testament) identifies it as one of the holy places. Sadly, it was at Gilgal where King Saul made a choice that marked the beginning of the end of his kingship.

Shortly after the celebration of Saul as king, the Philistines, who would be Saul's lifetime nemesis, declared war against Israel (1 Samuel 13:1-15). They had vastly superior numbers, and the Hebrews were cowering in fear. Saul panicked as well. His fear of losing the support of Israel, coupled with Samuel's delay in coming to meet him at Gilgal, prompted him to offer sacrifices to the Lord without Samuel being present. When Samuel reached Gilgal and saw what had been done, he was more than indignant.

Saul's thoughts and actions were a grave offense to Samuel and to the Lord. His specific offense was a willful disobedience of Samuel's instructions (1 Samuel 10:8). Though this may seem to be a minor infraction, it indicated a heart that did not respect Samuel's role or trust Samuel's words. Of course, in violating Samuel's word, Saul was actually violating God's will. Saul acted presumptuously.

This would not be the only time that Saul saw fit to do things in his own way. As the narrative further reveals, Saul disobeyed the Lord a second time. He was instructed by the Lord to utterly destroy the Amalekites as God's judgment for their sin. However, Saul refused to follow this command. Instead, he showed cowardice in allowing the demands of the people to overcome his obligation to carry out God's command (1 Samuel 15:24), and this resulted in God's rejecting Saul's kingship (1 Samuel 15:1-34).

Saul's life continued to spiral downward from that point. He would never regain favor with the Lord. He would see and come to know his successor, David. When the Spirit of the Lord left Saul, a distressing spirit from the Lord entered him. This spirit vexed his soul until his very end. A promising start for dynastic rule and victory ended in tragedy. Saul and his three sons would die on the battlefield, and David would go on to enjoy the great promise of God for a dynastic rule extending to the coming of

Christ Jesus (1 Samuel 31:1-13; 2 Samuel 7:1-17; Acts 2:22-36). Saul's life is truly among the saddest in biblical history.

Lessons for Worship

The experience of Saul with the Lord provides poignant and painful lessons for us regarding worship. The most critical of these lessons centers in understanding what worship really is. For most, worship is a public act inclusive of various rituals. Saul's life demonstrated this view of worship. The glaring problem with this view is that it misses worship as an act of life. His plan for Saul was for him to lead His people, and had Saul done this as commanded, it would have been an act of worship in itself. When Paul wrote to the Christians in Rome, he described worship in the sense of a life endeavor and not an occasional ritual (Romans 12:1-2). He wrote about the transformation of the mind as a means of daily character development demonstrated in daily godly conduct. King Saul never grasped this. The actions of his life demonstrate this.

First, Saul's actions revealed that he considered worship as a means to a more important end. Samuel's clear instructions to Saul were to wait at Gilgal for Samuel to offer sacrifices to God before Saul would go into battle. He was to wait seven days. When Samuel did not arrive on the seventh day in what Saul considered to be a timely manner, Saul foolishly offered the sacrifices himself. He had panicked and feared going to battle without this act of worship. Rather than having his heart devoted to the Lord as the essence of worship, he saw sacrificial offerings as his assurance of victory. His concern was not that of being devoted to the Lord. Rather, it was on currying favor from the Lord.

We must ask ourselves what is it that really motivates our worship. For some, coming to a public assembly or having personal times of devotion are done as means of seeking favor. There can be the hope of a new job, a better living situation, a marriage-leading relationship, or even better health. These are not thoughts of true worship. These are the thoughts often linked to pagan rites. The thought is that of appeasing the gods

Chapter Seven

so that doors will be opened to better gains in this life. We must remember that worship is not to be motivated by a mere desire to curry God's favor. Rather, a daily walk with God, centered in wanting to live for Him in appreciation of His love toward us, is at the heart of worship. Does God show favor to faithful, consecrated living? Yes, He often does. Is it wrong to enjoy such blessings? Certainly not. Should we expect these as a reward for our sincere devotion to Him? Not necessarily. It is true that Scripture speaks to divine favor for the faithful (Psalm 1). However, it is equally true that the faithful followers can be and often are those who suffer the most (1 Peter 4:16). Succinctly put, we can and should enjoy the favor that God graciously affords us. However, drawing closer to Him should not be motivated by a mere desire for the nicer things in life. Saul did gain victory, but he lost the spiritual war in the process.

A second cautionary lesson from Saul regards the primacy of worship. We gain this lesson from observing Saul's actions of defeating the Amalekites (1 Samuel 15:1-21). Saul experienced victory over the Amalekites, but he did so without regard to God's command. After this victory, he went to Carmel to set up a self-promoting memorial. From there, he went to Gilgal with the stated intention of offering sacrifices to the Lord (1 Samuel 15:15).

This was the second time that Saul seemed to have had it all backwards. In the first instance, he placed a desire for victory over life-devotion to the Lord. In the second instance, he placed self-aggrandizement over the divine source of his victory. Saul simply could not get out of his own shadow. He stood in the way of getting himself to God.

When our lives are lived as an act of worship, we will always thirst for special moments of worship. Our days will start and end with a recognition of all that God has done in bringing us into and through a new day. We will thank Him in the morning and the evening for the movement of every limb, the function of every internal organ, the blessing of every external capability, and the joy of every victory we have (Psalm 92:1-2). God's enabling will be the thought behind all that we have accomplished. Our monument, our boast will be in what He has done through us (Philippians 4:13). Nor will our praise be on those daily good experiences alone. They will also be offered in times of anguish and grief. Even in those times, we will not build monuments of helplessness and pity. Instead, we will look to Him to deliver us in His good timing (Psalm 55:16-17). We must always remember that public and private worship—as both the core of life and the ritual we perform—are to be of primary importance in our lives.

A third admonitory lesson from the life of King Saul is to keep others from standing in the way of our worship of God. This lesson, as are all of them, points to both our acts of worship as well as living for God as an act of worship.

Samuel had the sad task of informing Saul of God's rejection of him as king. When he met with Saul after the victory over the Amalekites, Samuel condemned his disobedience (1 Samuel 15:13-23). After attempts to excuse his behavior, Saul confessed to his sin (1 Samuel 15:24). As could have been predicted from the self-doubt he showed from the beginning, Saul allowed other people to color his picture of God.

Perhaps one of the clearest indicators of our picture of God is how we react to what others have to say about it. We are not told the details of the conversation over the spoils of war. Was Saul initially holding firm against the desires of the people to keep some of the treasures? Did he reveal to them what God had commanded, or was he too fearful to do so? Was he adamant about this total destruction as representative of his dedication to the Holy One of Israel, or was he ashamed to state this? Did he ever really see himself as God's warrior? Though his actions can substantiate any number of these possibilities, his excuse was a fear of the people.

Each of us must ask ourselves what negative impact others have on our worship. More importantly, we must ask ourselves if others are having a negative impact on our relationship with God. With regard to our corporate worship, it is entirely possible to stifle our emotions and the true expressions of our hearts to avoid negative judgment. We can become so engrossed in how we look

Chapter Seven

to others that we swallow our praise in the name of supposed proper worship conduct. The danger of this is to leave ourselves feeling empty and spiritually frustrated. Although worship is not to be thoughtless, it is also not to be emotionless. We cannot allow others to get in the way of our worshiping God. This also applies to our private, personal devotions. Some Christians fear that others will frown upon or ridicule a regular personal devotion routine. Whether it's private or public worship, the fear of negative labeling can chase us away from our expressions of devotion. They need not do so. God is to be praised and entreated no matter what others may think, say, or do.

A final troubling lesson from Saul must be learned. When we fail to honor God as a daily act of worship, we become subject to a distressing spirit (1 Samuel 16:14). Saul was never the same after his rejection. Where he previously enjoyed the benefit of having the Spirit of God come upon him, he later suffered the results of having a distressing spirit from the Lord visit him.

How are we to understand what happened to Saul? It would be a mistake to consider that he simply began to experience a mental and emotional breakdown as easily described by modern-day behavior science. We cannot travel the path of demystifying the text. The Scriptures testify to a dimension of reality unseen by us but no less real (Ephesians 2:1-2). When we consider the sovereignty of God and His subsequent power to limit the demonic world, we come to a plausible explanation. Because of Saul's rebelliousness, God allowed Saul to be distressed by a demonic spirit. Perhaps the concept found in one of Jesus' teachings can help us to understand what occurred with Saul (Matthew 12:43-45). Regardless, the point to be made it that his rebellious spirit opened him to the influence of a demonic spirit, which drove him to madness. It drove him to seek David's life and the life of his own son (1 Samuel 18:10-11; 20:17-34).

When we understand worship to be a matter of life as opposed to a matter of regular ritual, we will see how vitally important it is to our mental and emotional well-being. There is something about having God at the center of life that keeps us properly balanced and focused on what life in this world is all about. In addition, an abiding sense of the reality of eternity helps us to avoid getting caught up in the things of time. No matter what we experience in this life, our walk with God, continuously renewed in worship, anchors our minds and stabilizes our souls.

Final Thoughts

The tragic case of King Saul leaves us much to consider about worship. God gave him the opportunity to rule His people, but he never allowed a love for God to rule his life. He never saw God's call to kingship as a call to a life of worship. We can read of his tragedy, but we need not follow in his steps.

For Further Thought

1. What do you think moved Saul from shyness to rebelliousness?
2. In what sense is a call to worship more than a call to an assembly?
3. How do we keep ourselves focused on worship as a way of life?
4. What makes a person worship God in lieu of having a real relationship with God?
5. How is this (question 4) demonstrated in Saul's life?
6. Why must worship be considered primary in our lives?
7. Why is our motivation for worship vitally important?
8. What are some ways in which others can negatively impact our sense and experience of worship?

Chapter Eight

Studies in Worship
David

Introduction
It is nearly impossible to think of the matter of worship without thinking of David. He is a larger-than-life character whose exploits are significantly covered in the Scriptures. He serves as a powerful teacher in instructing us on what it means to worship our Lord.

The Man Who Would Be King
David's description from early on was to be borne out later (1 Samuel 16:18). However, from the start, one could see the strength of character based on how he had carried out his shepherding role. Saul was eager to accept David as his armor bearer.

David's heroics were put on display early as he slew the 9'2" giant, Goliath. He showed his zeal for the Lord in his reaction to Goliath's challenge (1 Samuel 17:26; 45-47). He showed his tenacious bravery in his response to Saul when seeking permission to battle Goliath (1 Samuel 17:31-37). Sadly, the slaying of Goliath would be the high point of David's relationship with King Saul (1 Samuel 18:5-16). The aftermath of this amazing feat made Saul suspicious and hateful of David until the end of Saul's life.

Drawing Nearer

It is in his flight for survival away from Saul that we gain more insight into David's spirit of worship. He sought out God's direction (1 Samuel 23:1-4). The ephod used in connection with seeking God's will was a garment worn by priests in sacerdotal service. David's continued flight was laced with opportunities to evade Saul's pursuit. He had chances to kill Saul, but he chose not to (1 Samuel 24:1-7; 26:1-25). He continued to flee from Saul. He surreptitiously joined forces with the Philistines on occasion to keep a safe distance from Saul. In the midst of all that he did to avoid capture by Saul, the Lord was leading him closer to his call to be officially recognized as Israel's king.

David's reluctant battles with Saul would come to a climatic end. After the Lord had thwarted and frustrated all of Saul's plans against David, Saul found himself in battle with his deadly enemies, the Philistines. He had become so unhinged that he sought a spiritualist to summon the deceased Samuel for an emergency consultation (1 Samuel 28:1-19). This turned out to be disastrous, and the ensuing battle turned out to be a fatal one for Saul and this sons (1 Samuel 31:1-13). David would be declared king among the house of Judah first, and eventually, by Israel as a whole (2 Samuel 5:1-5). He was 30 years old at that point, and he would be blessed to rule over God's people for 40 years.

David's pre-kingship years reveal him to be God-focused even while growing into manhood. He was certainly aware of God's presence and activity in his affairs during those years. His kingship years put his life-worship perspective in even sharper view. He continued to seek the Lord's counsel for his governmental decisions (2 Samuel 5:17-25). He would bring the Ark of God into the City of David (southern Jerusalem) to pay homage to the Lord (2 Samuel 6:1-23). He would then make his most notable decision—that of seeking to build a "house" for the Lord (2 Samuel 7:1-17). This desire of David was greatly honoring to the Lord. It revealed more of David's heart for the Lord, and it resulted in a covenantal promise to David that yet remains with us to this day through Christ Jesus (Acts 2:29-36). David would go on to firmly establish his kingdom. He had the favor of God and secure status

Chapter Eight

as king. This period of his life was the zenith of David's story with the Lord. Sadly, this was not the end of his story.

The infamous episode of David and Bathsheba nearly permanently derailed David's story. We are told that it occurred at a time after the winter or rainy season. This was a time when military campaigns would resume (2 Samuel 11:1). David did not go out with his troops, and this gave opportunity for him to break faith with God's law. This act of adultery was further advanced to an act of murder as a means of covering what David thought was a secret sin (2 Samuel 11:2-27). For this brief moment in his life, David's life-worship perspective was eclipsed by his fleshly desires. Thankfully, his heart was re-centered on the Lord (2 Samuel 12:1-15). However, this episode permanently changed the trajectory of David's life.

The calamities that visited David were enough to make any person cringe. First, there was the death of the son that he and Bathsheba conceived (2 Samuel 12:16-19). Next, there was the dastardly sexual abuse that David's son, Amnon, committed against David's daughter, Tamar (2 Samuel 13:1-22), an act that ignited no less than a civil war. David's son, Absalom, avenged Tamar by killing Amnon (2 Samuel 13:23-33). Absalom fled from David but later returned. However, he still harbored deep resentment for David. His anger at his father's failure to exercise justice in the crime against Tamar, coupled with his father's unwillingness to see him for two years after his return, boiled into stealthy anarchy (2 Samuel 14:1—15:37). Absalom temporarily deposed David, publicly humiliating him, and forcing David to leave Jerusalem (2 Samuel 16:15-23). Absalom's rebellion proved to be short-lived as the ensuing battle between loyalists to David and loyalists to Absalom played out (2 Samuel 18:1-33). Though David won the battle, he lost the war in the sense that Absalom was killed. The melancholy that overtook him remained with him for the rest of his life.

David's final phase of life found him secured as Israel's king but greatly wearied by continued wars (2 Samuel 21:1-22). He had put down yet another rebellion (2 Samuel 20:1-25), but more trouble was to come. He suffered the discipline of God in conducting a census of the nation (2 Samuel 24:1-25). The sin in this action was found in David's self-exaltation. He came to evaluate his power as being based in the number of his subjects.

David's final days still included a degree of trial. There was controversy over his successor (1 Kings 1:5-52). After securing Solomon as his successor, David's day came to an end (1 Kings 2:10). He left behind an amazing story of the tremendous heights and the darkest depths possible when a man or woman seeks to walk with the Lord.

Lessons for Worship

Where should one attempt to start in learning worship lessons from David? His life was so rich in experience with the Lord that it is hard to know where to begin. Perhaps the best place for us to start is with the recognition that David saw all of life as worship. He shows us that worship of God is not merely done within the confines of a sanctuary. Rather, it includes seeking after Him in making our day-to-day decisions (1 Samuel 23:1-12; 30:1-8; 2 Samuel 2:1). Every worship lesson that we learn from David centers on the fact that the Lord was the center of his life.

The covenants that David made with Jonathan reveal his sense of worship (1 Samuel 20:35-42; 23:14-18). Again, he saw nothing outside of God's vision, and he acted accordingly—except in the case of Uriah and Bathsheba. This shows how we must live all of life as worship. Our understanding of worship must be that the Lord always sees us. Nothing is hidden from Him. When we are engaged in transactions with persons on our jobs or in our communities, our behavior is under the scope of God. When we are dealing with one another in our homes, we are still in God's sight. When we are interacting with family members and even in our times of solitude, our Lord sees us. Our coming to Christ places us under His ownership. Our lives are not our own. We have committed ourselves to be living sacrifices to the Lord. Our worship then must be a life engagement. Even though this can be troubling, it is really only troubling when we are tempted to

Chapter Eight

behave outside of the parameters of God's will. It is not as though the Lord functions as a divine policeman looking to flag us down at every infraction of the law. Instead, we have entered into this Divine-human relationship of a love-obligation that causes us to think about our behavior for the sake of love. This is the spirit that controls all our dealings with others. Such life worship is more praiseworthy than merely singing a song from a hymnal.

Another instance revealing David's all-encompassing attitude of worship was seen in his sparing Saul's life. Rather than recklessly and disrespectfully take advantage of these opportunities to kill his enemy, David allowed his sense of God's presence to keep him from such actions. Along life's path, we have and will encounter situations in which we are the innocent victims of ill treatment. These can be instances of unfair treatment in the home, on the job, or in any random encounter with people. Life has a way of opening opportunities for us to avenge ourselves of such instances of ill treatment. These are times in which our faith in God's means of redressing such injustices is put to the test. Our flesh calls on us to "get even" and to add a bit more just for good measure. However, a sense of life-worship can prevent us from such actions. It will caution us against seeing that not all opportunities to right the wrongs against us are God-created. It will remind us that God avenges us in ways that are just (1 Samuel 24:12). Living life as an act of worship will free us from misguided attempts to operate in the flesh in the name of the Spirit (Romans 12:17-19; James 1:19-20).

The youthful years of David present yet another worship lesson for us. His story shows us the value of developing a heart for God in our youth. Although we do not have clear insight into what David learned as a youth in Jesse's household, we can be sure that respect for the Lord God was emphasized. Such grounding in youthful years prepares the soil for a life of worship. Some of us can recall Christian hymns from our yesteryears. We can remember elements of worship services regularly attended in our youth. For many, these are warm memories of comforting times within the cocoon of imperfect but loving people seeking to follow Jesus. It is amazing how much these childhood experiences prepared us for a life of worship. Other people who never had that experience came to know the Lord later in life. In many instances, these persons have children whom they rear with the inclusion of regular worship service attendance. The value of such can never be fully measured.

We do well to place great priority on exposing children to worship. Our world continues to push against such practice, and it does so at the detriment of our youth. Children need exposure to praising the Lord, learning His Word, communicating with Him in prayer, and all other elements and aspects of worship. They need instruction in the home on the importance of respect for Him in their day-to-day behavior. If we are concerned with ensuring that our children learn the practical skills to function in life, we must be equally or even more concerned that they be exposed to life before the Lord. Exposing them to worship regularly opens them to seeing life as God-centered. Like David, they can have the opportunity to live the fullness of their lives with the Divine center that guides them from "cradle to grave."

David's rise to power reveals many instances of divine and human favor. This aspect of David's life provides us with further principles regarding worship. As with other worship lessons from David, this one flows from his life-worship mentality. Once Samuel anoints David as king, the Spirit of God came upon him, and instances of divine favor rest upon him. Yet, before this event, God's favor rested upon David. He was kept safe in his slaying of a lion and a bear (1 Samuel 17:34-36). This is no everyday experience. Though perhaps not a miraculous thing, it was still indicative of God's hand upon David. One can surmise that there were other such indications of God's pre-anointing favor upon David. He being a man after God's heart was something that David had fixed himself on from his youth. In whichever way it was provided to him, David accepted and dedicated himself to the way of the Holy One of Israel in his youth. This life-worship mindset proved to be the conduit of God's favor. It was also the avenue of human favor.

Chapter Eight

When we speak of human favor, we are speaking about how others are kindly disposed toward us. These are persons who are not necessarily fellow Christians or other friends. Rather, this can include those who are our known or unknown enemies (Proverbs 16:17). Though we expect our friends to be favorable to us, it is our enemies' or a stranger's kindness to us that serves as a reward of a life-worship. There is something about a God-fearing and life-as-worship-centered person that attracts favor from some of the most ungodly living persons that we encounter. Be it on the job, at the places we do business, or among the people in our community, human favor is extended to us in the most unlikely ways. This is both a God-thing and a human-thing in that God's providence is working in our lives by means of such persons making free-will choices to bless us. David saw this occur even among a Philistine king (1 Samuel 27:1-12; 29:6). We can and do experience this in various walks of life. When we are living with a life-worship mindset, we are opening ourselves to God's opening of the windows of heaven to us (Malachi 3:10). Maintaining a life-worship lifestyle will result in divine and some human favor.

A final lesson regarding worship comes to us from David. When we lose a life-worship perspective, we expose ourselves to deep sorrows. There is a sad footnote to the life of David. It concerns his dastardly deed against Uriah (2 Samuel 11:1-27). It was an episode in David's life that haunted him for the rest of his life. Though he found God's grace in this situation, he also found the unpredictable consequences of his sin. His lapse from a life-worship mindset produced truly disastrous results.

There is good reason for maintaining a life-worship mindset. Such a mindset about worship can literally save our lives. When we live life as an act of worship and make our decisions in life from that perspective, we will continually prosper (Psalm 1:1-3). This is not the falsely claimed experience of the popular "prosperity gospel." True prosperity is not based upon material or even temporal things. Rather, it is the satisfaction of the soul in union with God. Here, there is no lack or want for the things that sustain life, for there is the confidence of God's provisions throughout life. To walk away from this is truly an act of sinning against ourselves (Psalm 1:4-6).

We do well to constantly discipline ourselves to stay in a life-worship mindset. Like we discipline ourselves to do things that we at times care not to do, so must we do to maintain a life-worship mindset. There is no better or other way to live life to its fullness.

Final Thoughts

Beginning and continuing our lives as an act of worship before the Lord will result in incomparable blessing. Such a mindset will serve as divinely painted road markers to guide us on our way as we travel through life. The journey will have its share of dangerous impediments, and the devil will always flash false detours. However, our daily life-as-worship mindset will keep us centered and properly focused as we make our way toward eternity.

For Further Thought

1. How does one develop a life-as-worship mindset?
2. What are some indicators that this was David's mindset from youth?
3. How does our attitude concerning worship help define our character?
4. What are some challenges to developing a life-as-worship mindset?
5. How do we best teach our children to develop such a mindset?
6. What are some examples of divine and human favor?
7. What experiences of divine and human favor in your life?
8. How did God's favor remain with David even after his fall with Bathsheba?

Chapter Nine
Studies in Worship
Jeroboam

Introduction
The death of King David began a slippery slope of danger for God's people. Solomon, David's heir to the throne, had polluted his soul with the worship of idol gods, and this impaired his judgment. This sad episode gave birth to the reign and ruin of Jeroboam.

The Reign of the Notorious King
Jeroboam entered the scene as an ambitious and industrious leader under Solomon (1 Kings 11:26-28). The Lord visited Jeroboam and revealed His plan for Jeroboam's life. Solomon's and the people's sin of idolatry had evoked God's judgment, and Jeroboam was called to lead God's people back to the right path (1 Kings 11:29-39). This man was offered the same blessings that God had pronounced and provided to David (1 Kings 11:38).

Drawing Nearer

The news of God's promise to Jeroboam somehow made its way to Solomon, and he, in turn, sought to kill Jeroboam (1 Kings 11:40). It is likely that Jeroboam's rebellion against Solomon was engendered by God's revelation to him through the prophet, Ahijah. Jeroboam likely saw this as an opportunity or even as sanction to lead an insurrection. Surely the economic woes of the people were a source of national frustration before Rehoboam ascended to the throne (1 Kings 12:1-4). Whatever the specific sequence of events, Jeroboam had fled to Egypt. However, his influence remained in Jerusalem, and his loyalists did not hesitate to encourage his return when Rehoboam became king (1 Kings 12:1-4; 2 Chronicles 10:1-4).

Rehoboam's reign began with a national revolt. The frustrated and stressed nation yearned for financial relief, and he chose to ignore the people's request. The result was a divided kingdom and the rise of the reign of Jeroboam as Israel's king (1 Kings 12:1-24). Jeroboam would become infamous in his acts to corrupt the worship of God.

Jeroboam's first act as king was to establish a rival worship location and an alternate worship ritual for Israel (1 Kings 12:25-33; 2 Chronicles 11:15). He gave no regard for the instructions that God have given for worship. He forsook the Lord's command against idolatry (Exodus 20:1-6). He abandoned God's law concerning the priesthood (2 Chronicles 11:13-14). He established worship centers in the high places—a reference regularly connected with pagan worship.

Jeroboam's decree for constructing golden calves caught the eye of Bible students. Such an action was reminiscent of Israel's sin in Moses' day. The golden calf was a popular religious figure in ancient Egyptian and Canaanite cultures. The common thought was that the creation of such images brought the god closer to the worshiper and even provided the worshiper a level of control. These golden calves, and all the idolatrous actions of the people under Jeroboam, led to the future destruction of the people and the extermination of the progeny of Jeroboam (1 Kings 13:33-34).

Chapter Nine

Having been warned of his foolish and apostate choice, Jeroboam refused to correct his path. Yet, when faced with the deadly illness of his son, Jeroboam sought God's messenger. The deceptive manner in which he did so revealed his guilt over his chosen path. The response to his inquiry was purely devastating. Not only would his son die, but his progeny would end (1 Kings 14:1-18).

The Scriptures record that Jeroboam's reign was consumed with battles against Judah (the Southern Kingdom) that ultimately ended with Jeroboam's demise (2 Chronicles 12:15; 13:1-19). He had never turned from his wicked and rebellious ways. He died in battle by the Lord's hand.

In retrospect, Jeroboam took a bad thing and made it worse. Solomon's introduction of idolatry set the nation on the wrong path. There is no indication that Rehoboam was out to rid the nation of these idolatrous practices (1 Kings 14:21-24; 2 Chronicles 12:15-16). Jeroboam had the opportunity to do so, but he failed miserably. In the end, he lost his son, his kingship, and his soul.

Lessons for Worship

There is something about a life even as tragic as Jeroboam's that holds a treasure of lessons for us. This is particularly the case as it concerns applicable lessons for worship. Unlike David, Jeroboam showed no heart for God and no sense of His wholly other nature. The predictable results were his establishment of a rival, but false, worship cult. Powerful and practical lessons must be considered from these choices.

Jeroboam's sad example teaches us that we must avoid a skewed sense of worship purpose. Failure to do so will lead to some predictable results. For Jeroboam, worship ceased to be about God and became more about his quest to retain power. Having tasted a level of authority under Solomon's reign, and having been chased from Jerusalem to Egypt, Jeroboam was only too eager to come back at the death of Solomon. He seized his opportunity to gain power, and he used worship to maintain that power. Much like many of today's ministering charlatans, Jeroboam's concern for religion was for keeping people under his rule so as to secure his kingship (1 Kings 12:25-27).

Whether a worship leader or a worship participant, the purpose of our worship can never be allowed to become skewed. We can never allow ourselves to seek to be the center of the worship. Again, this is a matter of concern for both worship leaders and participants. As a leader, one can be so fixated on having the spotlight that he sings, preaches, prays, or speaks for show. There can be a mingled sense satisfying a need for personal attention. This can happen unconsciously. We all bring our personal baggage into the Lord's kingdom. Your failures in life, my perceived slights from others, and our need for validation can creep into the forefront of our minds and taint our actions in worship. A preacher's sermon can become his opportunity for adulation and personal gratification. The audience is impressed, excited, and/or entertained. The people are enamored by his gifted speech. This response plays into his deep need for affection, acceptance, and validation. He begins to think less about preaching as an act of setting God before the people and more about setting up himself. This gradually leads to a desperation to say or do anything to sustain this egotistical high. Sadly, God is forced behind the curtain, and the show goes on. The preacher is in a never-ending quest to maintain his sense of control over, support of, and/or superficial allegiance of the congregants.

This can be the story of a song leader, music minister, class teacher, small groups leader, preacher, or any other person serving in a church leadership capacity. It is all too easy for anyone in such a position to become a modern-day Jeroboam as pertains to worship. We can fall into the same trap from the stage or in the pew. My voice has to outshine yours. Your lesson-response has to outshine mine. Our praise report has to be more dramatic or death-defying than everyone else's. These all fall under the category of skewing the purpose of worship.

Chapter Nine

If the focus of worship is not laser-focused on the Lord, then it is vain worship. He is to be the center of everything that we do in a worship service. We do not engage in worship to promote ourselves. Rather, we are to engage in worship because God is worthy of it. We are not to worship the Lord for some personal advantage or benefit. It is simply because God is worthy. He's worthy of our time, our attention, and our devotion. Jeroboam somehow got it twisted. Let us not do the same.

Jeroboam's fall was also wrapped around a desire to accommodate the comforts and conveniences of the people as pertains to worship. He reasoned that it was too inconvenient for them to travel back to Jerusalem to worship as God had specified. In his duplicity, he placed the people's comfort before proper worship.

Worship is not about the worshiper. In our crazed attempts to adjust to our current cultural, generational shift, we see churches doing all that they can to please the worshiper. Unlike Jeroboam, we cannot afford to think that worshiping the God of heaven requires no scrutiny of what we do. We have not been given a blank slate on which to write any action or ritual that we think to please an audience. Worship is an audience of one, and it is imperative that this One is pleased in what we offer.

Christianity is in another uniquely challenging world today. The cultural shifts of our time have churches torn. For example, we are again struggling with what role our women should have in the local church. American culture demands gender equality—as well it should. However, equality in the mind of popular culture is not necessarily equivalent with the Scriptures. God's justice demands a stand for equality of pay for women in the same job as a man. So too for job opportunities, political office, or other areas of human endeavor. However, God's Word remains unchanged in His instructions for church function. The instruction is for men to lead the local church (1 Timothy 2:1-15; 3:1-7). The Lord has never made a distinction in the worth and value of His human creation, but He has made some distinction in some of the functions of male and female. Further, even though all are one in Christ Jesus (Galatians 3:26-28), men and women do not have the same assigned roles within the local church. We are causing ourselves much harm in seeking to accommodate new cultural gender norms in the local church. We must remember that such norms continue to shift. Once we begin trying to please society in one thing, we will have opened ourselves to doing so in further things. With the amount of gender debate and confusion prevalent today, churches need to exercise extreme care. We do not want to be guilty of inviting others to Bethel and Dan (1 Kings 12:28-29).

Jeroboam's encounter with the younger prophet of God brings us yet another worship lesson (1 Kings 13:1-10). God, through the prophet, pronounced condemnation upon Jeroboam for his wicked actions. Though he was performing an acceptable act of worship (burning incense), his worship was condemned. Worship can never be acceptable when the heart and the deed are not in alignment with God's will.

As we have seen is several examples, worshiping God has everything to do with the heart of the worshiper. It is never about our rituals in and of themselves. God's concern is for the condition of our hearts. Jeroboam well knew that he was operating outside of God's instruction for worship. Golden calves could never represent the true God, and no amount of incense burning could mask the repugnant smell of idolatry. Today, the idols are different, but their stench is still the same.

The tragic reign of Jeroboam offers us a final lesson. In seeking to secure his hold over the people by reconstructing their worship, he indiscriminately selected priests (1 Kings 12:32; 13:33). He gave no regard for God's direction for the priests. His violations of God's law concerning the priesthood were so offensive to the Levites that they left from under his rule (2 Chronicles 11:13-17).

We can never acquiesce to false worship practices without becoming corrupt worshipers. Surely the priests who left were offended by their rejection, but the indication is that their move was not merely one of personal rejection. They saw it as an offense before the Lord. This reminds us that introducing elements to our worship that have no scriptural foundation is offensive to God. For us to continue to practice things that violate God's instruction for worship is dangerous. Although we never want to become dogmatic in what is considered acceptable and unacceptable worship practices, we never should acquiesce to any practice without a solid scriptural foundation. These can be very tricky waters to navigate. It has become significantly unpopular to raise the issue of proper and improper worship. The pendulum has swung from dogmatic stances based in racial, cultural, and generational understandings to a violent rejection of the need to ask the question of acceptable practices. It seems as if popular culture is the tail wagging the dog. It is truly a dangerous time for the church, and we need to use Jeroboam's story to be up for the challenge.

Final Thoughts

One of the many beautiful things about the Bible is its honesty. No character is made more or less than what he or she really was. In Jeroboam, we find a man who seemingly had great promise but allowed power and pride to take him down the wrong path. This should impress upon us the need for developing a God-centered life. Such a life will always force us to seek the Lord's counsel for how we think, how we worship, and how we live.

Drawing Nearer

For Further Thought

1. What are some positive qualities initially seen in Jeroboam?
2. What brought about Jeroboam's reign?
3. How did Jeroboam's religious action impact the nation?
4. What are some idols that people worship today?
5. Why is it so difficult to discuss proper worship rituals in the church today?
6. How can we best determine God's instruction for acceptable worship practices?
7. How do we best address congregational controversies over proper worship?
8. How can culture negatively impact the church's worship?

Chapter Ten

Studies in Worship
Isaiah

Introduction
God's prophets are a fascinating collection of characters. Each was called into a time and situation that required a special word from the Lord. Isaiah came during a time of crisis. It is in this call that we gain a powerful picture of worship.

The Call of Isaiah
Isaiah's career spanned the reign of four kings of Judah (Isaiah 1:1). He was called by the Lord long after God's people had split into the Northern and Southern Kingdoms. Isaiah was an urban dweller who was quite used to life in the city of Jerusalem. He was the son of Amoz (Isaiah 1:1), who rabbinic tradition holds to be the brother of King Amaziah. This would mean that Isaiah was first cousin to King Uzziah and part of the royal family, which gives us insight into his seemingly ease of access to the king and his court.

Isaiah was a family man with a wife and two sons. His message was one of impending judgment and ultimate hope. Each of his sons was given a name predictive of the future of the nation of Judah (Isaiah 7:3; 8:3). God decreed that the nation would be overtaken by a foreign power, but a remnant of the nation would be saved. The prophet boldly proclaimed God's message.

Drawing Nearer

The setting of Isaiah's call is critical to our understanding his mission. It was in the year 740 BC, the year Uzziah died, that he received his call. Israel, the Northern Kingdom, was to fall to Assyria in 722 BC. Israel had already been experiencing some turmoil. However, Judah had experienced a revival of power and prominence under the reign of King Uzziah. The king had been enjoying a 52-year reign. His ascent to the throne began with his being a co-regent with his father, Amaziah, who was a good king, but had not eliminated idolatrous practices from Judah (2 Kings 14:1-4). He also foolishly entered into battle with Israel and was soundly defeated (2 Kings 14:8-14; 2 Chronicles 25:20-24). After Amaziah's death, the people proclaimed Uzziah as king over Judah (2 Chronicles 26:1).

Uzziah inherited a weakened nation, but God was with him (2 Chronicles 26:3-15). Under his reign, the military was made strong. Trade and commerce brought about significant prosperity. Building and construction were the norms of the era. In all, it was a stable and prosperous time. Sadly, such a time provided fertile ground for the development of a God-forsaking spirit.

As had happened with God's people in previous eras, ease gave way to unfaithfulness. God witnessed His people's turn from humility to arrogance. Uzziah had become prideful and arrogant, and this led to God's judgment on him. He was stricken with leprosy and had to spend the last of his days away from his throne (2 Chronicles 26:16-23). In addition, the nation's sinfulness was on full display. The wealthy took advantage of the poor—building their wealth at the expense of the poor. The justice system had become perverted in favor of the rich and powerful. Greed was the norm, and materialism was boldly flaunted. Religion had become a farce. The people performed rituals and stepped through religious formalities with no concern for godly behavior. This deplorable spiritual condition is aptly described in the opening of Isaiah's prophecy (Isaiah 1:1-31). The Lord would not abide this state of unfaithfulness any further, so Isaiah was called to declare God's coming judgment and His mercy on those who would repent.

Chapter Ten

God often demonstrates His lordship in His involvement in human affairs. Judah's coming crisis was no exception. As Judah was enjoying its time of prosperity, God reawakened the Assyrian nation. Its lust for power and conquest was rekindled, and Assyria began to look to the west for new nations to conquer. The Assyrians had already engaged in campaigns against some of Judah's neighboring nations. In 740 BC, the Assyrians set their sight on Israel and Judah. Assyria's conquest campaign would play out over the next few years. As the Northern Kingdom saw the Assyrian threat, it sought to fortify itself against Assyrian aggression. The Northern Kingdom formed an alliance with neighboring Syria. The Southern Kingdom was urged to join the alliance, but it had refused. War broke out between these nations and the encroaching Assyrians (Syro-Ephraimitic war of 734 BC). Judah, under duress from Israel and Syria, foolishly reached out to the Assyrians for deliverance (2 Kings 16:1-18). He capitulated to the demands of the Assyrians in hopes of receiving Assyria's help in battle against Israel and Syria. This was as fruitless as it was foolish, and it ended in disaster (2 Chronicles 28:22-25). The Lord was acting in all of these affairs in bringing judgment against Judah (2 Kings 15:32—17:20). Isaiah was actively prophesying throughout these troubled years.

At Isaiah's call, the aforementioned tragedies were on the horizon. He would live to see all this unfold. His reference to Uzziah's death is quite poignant. It was in that year that he saw the Lord! Was his recognition of the Lord in this special sense the result of the loss of a family member? Did the foreboding sense of international crisis overcome him and force him to look beyond the power of a human monarch? Was God making use of all this to get Isaiah's attention? Each of these factors resonates with the context.

From this unearthly experience of Isaiah's call and commission, we are granted uplifting and sobering lessons concerning our concept and experience of worship. Unlike God's people of old, we can never allow these lessons to fall on dull ears.

Lessons for Worship

A *theophany* is a manifestation of God by a means that humans can grasp. It is an ethereal experience. It is what Isaiah experienced as described by his word, "I saw the Lord" (Isaiah 6:1). The Scriptures declare to us that no human has seen God, because God is Spirit (John 4:24; 1 John 4:12). Moses wanted to see God, but he was denied. He was only allowed to see the back of God, which is an anthropomorphism to help convey the concept of God's perfect holiness. God hid Moses in the cleft of the rock for Moses' survival (Exodus 33:18-23).

It should be noted that some scholars believe that Isaiah actually saw the pre-incarnate Jesus sitting on the throne (John 12:37-41). Given John's description of Jesus in the opening of John's Gospel, it is plausible that Isaiah did see the pre-incarnate Christ. Also, there is an Aramaic paraphrase (*Targum*) of this text (Isaiah 6:1) that reads, "I saw the glory of the Lord." However, this chapter is focused on Isaiah as having seen a representation of God as Moses did. This consistency seems to make for the best understanding, though the other cannot be completely dismissed. In either understanding, the lessons concerning worship are validated.

When we think of worship from Isaiah's perspective, we can define *worship* as an experience of seeing God. As previously stated, no human can see God. However, worship can still be defined as an intense yearning to see Him. Like Moses, it is our longing to see beyond a manifestation of Him. Our souls desire complete union with Him. Like Moses, we want to have the chasm between the Holy God and sinful humanity completely closed. In this life, worship is an expression of that yearning to see God, be with Him, and have complete union with Him.

The history of humanity reveals this desire to see God. Since the fall of man in the Garden of Eden, humanity has expressed an innate sense of wanting union and communion with his Creator. Paul proclaimed this fact when addressing the audience on the Areopagus (Acts 17:26-28). We can observe this in the epochs of human history. Each one has always included some form of

Chapter Ten

worship or yearning for deeper meaning in life. Man is designed to be a worshiping creature, and our spirits are restless until they find union with our Creator. The devil is well aware of this, and he continues to offer some substitute as the object of humanity's worship. Every idol ever made, whether it be an inanimate thing or an elevated fallen creature, is the result of satanic deception. The devil takes the genuine need of humanity and twists that need to seek something made rather than the One who made all. This is the tragedy of idol worship. The innate need for worship is stifled in foolish bait-and-switch schemes.

We must understand that worship is essential to our very being. Another satanic ploy is to convince us that worship is really about God's need for our adoration. This deception is designed to twist our view of God as being a needy being, egotistically desirous of our attention. The reality is that we need Him, and not that He needs us. The Godhead is complete in itself. The creation of man is not based in God's need for human adoration and affection.

As we think about worship, we can praise our Lord Jesus for opening the opportunity for humanity to satisfy his innate longing. It is only through Christ that we have open access to the Father. Through Him, we can come boldly to the throne of grace (Hebrews 4:16-18). Through Him, our worship grants us a foretaste of this post-Eden desire of being reunited with the Godhead. It is true that we come into this union in baptism (Matthew 28:18-20). However, the full experience of being in union with God will not come until we are with Him in eternity. This earthly tabernacle with all of its subjectivity to fallen nature must be completely shed. We cannot see Him face-to-face in this age. However, there is a day coming when we will see Him in glory. The best that human descriptions can do is speak of a time when tears, sadness, pain, and death are outlawed (Revelation 21:4). The best picture that human language can convey is that of streets of gold and a city of precious stones (Revelation 21:14-21). The reality cannot even be expressed in words. It is this yearning for being in the midst of our God, and all that is involved with that experience, that earthly worship is wrapped around. We want to see Him. We yearn to be with Him. We cry out with our hearts toward this end. In every opportunity for worship, we want to see the Lord.

Isaiah's experience goes further in teaching us about worship. Worship is not only a desire to see God, but it also involves seeing God in the right way. Isaiah did not just see the Lord. He was more descriptive than that. He saw Him sitting on a throne (Isaiah 6:1). This in itself was a tremendous comfort for Isaiah. Uzziah, in whom Judah had come to place tremendous hope and trust, was gone. Assyria, sniffing weakness in the region, was going to be a force to be reckoned with. Closer, smaller, yet still threatening nations were near Judah. However, in the midst of all of this, it was God sitting on the throne.

Worship is our opportunity to have our perspective reoriented. In times of personal trial and hopelessness, national crisis and upheaval, and international uncertainty and calamity, we must see God sitting on the throne. We must refocus on His sovereignty. We must be reminded that He is in control. David so beautifully described this as being delivered from thoughts of an unjust world once he came into the sanctuary of God (Psalm 73). Worship allows us the opportunity to see all of life as under the ultimate control of our beneficent, just, sovereign, and loving God.

Isaiah also saw God as high and lifted up (Isaiah 6:1). This is a reference to the majestic nature of God's rule. The scene of God's majesty is amplified further in the description of the ruler's train filling the entire temple. The splendor of the Lord's robe was so awe-inspiring that it left no room for anyone to stand in the temple. What a powerful description! Again, the limitations of human language cannot do justice in fully conveying what Isaiah saw. Still, we are able to grasp the concept of God's glory being so intense that no human can stand in His presence. We can no more fully see the majesty of God than we can stare directly at the sun, and we are millions of miles away from something that our majestic God created from nothing!

Isaiah saw seraphim attending to Him who sat on His throne. These were hovering with two wings each as well as

Chapter Ten

covering their faces and bodies (feet) with two wings. The latter was showing reverential awe in the presence of God's glory. Comparing this scene with Ezekiel's vision, the covering of feet is the covering of the body (Ezekiel 1:11). The very praise that the seraphim uttered was enough to shake the building and fill the temple with smoke. In all, this is an unmistakable scene of due reverence for the Lord.

Worship is our opportunity to see the Lord's majesty. The term (worship) itself is wrapped around the thought of appropriate recognition of the one being worshiped. Isaiah's description of the Lord is how we must see Him. In our day of Christian consumerism, this is a much-needed lesson. Christianity is being promoted from the standpoint of churches seeking to attract customers. Like department stores, supermarkets, and online businesses, churches are looking for the right angle, the right bait, and the right pitch to make to potential consumers to get them to buy what we are selling. However, the Christian message is not to be merchandised. We are not called to "sell Jesus" to an indifferent or marginally interested world. We are called to call a lost and dying world to repent and believe in the gospel (Mark 1:15). We need to see the Lord's majesty to remember our sheer privilege to come before Him. We do Him no favors in coming to worship Him. Rather, worship is a privilege and an honor. We are actually allowed to come into the presence of the King!

Worship involves another component. It is that of how we see ourselves (Isaiah 6:5-7). Isaiah's immediate reaction to God's presence was a humbled recognition of his sinfulness. His cry of being undone was equivalent to saying that he was lost. His sense of lostness was not just because of being an inferior being in the presence of the wholly other God (Exodus 34:20). It was also because as a fallen human creature, he was also one of unclean lips. Understood as one unworthy to join in the praise that he witnessed, as one unworthy of carrying a divine message, or as one who's moral and ethical impurity has no right to be in the presence of the immaculate One, Isaiah was expressing who he was. It was an inherent call for cleansing.

Drawing Nearer

Genuine worship is inextricably tied to who we consider ourselves to be. This is why worship is a privilege. Far from thinking that God should be happy that we have come to worship Him, genuine worship involves a deep sense of thankfulness and humility that the Lord would allow us into His presence. We come to Him like the tax collector of Jesus' parable (Luke 18:10-14). We come bare before Him in gratitude that we can come at all.

If we are ever going to know pure worship, we have to shed attitudes of worthiness and casual, familiar approaches. I fear that the popular emphasis on the love of God has unwittingly promoted a lack of reverence for God and a lack of recognition of our sinfulness. Though it is true that He welcomes us to come to Him as our Father, it is equally true that we remember that He is our Father. The Lord is not our casual, familiar buddy and chum. This statement is not to promote an austere mechanical worship experience nor is it an attempt to dismiss the allowance of cultural and even generational expressions of worship. However, we must always realize that we are approaching the Holy One. No worship devoid of clarity of who He is and who and what we are, and the requisite humility and respect that this recognition demands, can ever be acceptable before Him.

Isaiah's experience impacts us with one final thought about our worship (Isaiah 6:8). In hearing the voice of the Lord concerning mission, Isaiah readily responded, "Here I am, send me!" These are familiar words to many Christians. They call us to remember that worship in this life is inextricably tied to mission.

For too many persons, worship is a fixation upon mere ethereal or emotional expression and feeling. America's Christian climate has been largely co-opted by self-focused philosophies of personal development and fulfillment. Worship planners seek to tap into this desire by promoting themselves as offering an atmosphere conducive for such experiences. This is really not a new phenomenon. The history of Christianity houses several epochs of the church being pulled into the cultural and philosophical streams of the day. However, genuine worship is never focused on mere self. Although there is a focus on self

Chapter Ten

in the sense of a call to godly living, it is never a call devoid of obligation to others.

Individual worship calls for us to consider our mission to those within our spheres of influence. Corporate worship should promote this same sense of mission for us as the local church. Family members, neighbors, coworkers, and others need a touch of God in their lives. There are families, schools, and communities that the Lord wants the local church to bless. Whenever our worship is devoid of a sense of duty to minister to these persons and systems, our worship is deficient.

We must also note that the mission is not necessarily one of human acceptance or even appreciation. Isaiah's task, given to him in a scene of worship, was not projected to be a pleasant one (Isaiah 6:9-13). Quite to the contrary, Isaiah's mission was painted in the colors of rejection and failure. Worship called him to duty, and duty was foretold to be fairly fruitless. As we grasp the connection of worship and mission, we do well to remember that the mission is not an easy one, and success cannot be measured by commonly held standards. Such standards are misleading when it comes to the mission for Christ.

It is interesting to see how Christianity is promoted today. In substance, popular Christianity is more about marketing an experience than it is about proclaiming the Christ. Churches have bought into securing the latest technological advancements and techniques that create a theatrical production to capture the imaginations of the audience. Too, the desired audience is the burgeoning unchurched of the country. The thought is that we must create the right physical, sensual atmosphere that will lock in the audience for approximately 30 minutes—inclusive of 10 minutes of a "Christian talk" that may or may not mention Jesus…let alone sin, obedience, repentance, and judgment. As numbers of attendees swell for such services, we deem this mission to be successful. This is certainly far afield from Isaiah's foretold experience. In reality, if Jesus is scripturally presented, standing-room-only crowds in our buildings will be more of the exception than the rule.

Final Thoughts

The great prophet Isaiah's call is one that brings powerful lessons to bear on our thoughts concerning worship. He helps us to see the need to seek union with God from our innermost being. He leaves us with the thought of being engaged with God in mission to the world. Worship and mission are symbiotically related. Worship feeds mission, and mission feeds worship. Each one fuses us closer and closer in union with the Lord.

For Further Thought

1. Why is belief in God's sovereignty so essential to our faith walk?
2. How can national or international calamities positively impact our faith?
3. What are some examples of how national or international crisis impacted the church?
4. How should God's nature impact our worship?
5. How should our view of ourselves impact our worship?
6. What is your definition of *mission*?
7. What is the connection between worship and mission?
8. In what ways are worship and mission symbiotic?

Chapter Eleven

Studies in Worship
Ezra

Introduction
The story of God's Old Covenant people is replete with the drama of Divine-human interaction and all that such interactions entail. There are constant disappointments, repeated failures, gracious promises, and bountiful mercies all captured in blatantly honest prose. From Ezra's time on the stage, we are presented with our final set of lessons on worship from this series of Old Testament characters.

The Priest Goes Home
The continuous cycle of obedience, rebellion, punishment, and forgiveness has reached its crescendo with the fall of Israel (722 BC) and Judah (586 BC). Israel, the Northern Kingdom, had allowed a corrupt king to introduce her to a path of destruction. Jeroboam's sin, and the people's acceptance of it, had taken them to utter destruction at the hands of Assyria (2 Kings 17:5-23). Judah's sin, even after seeing Israel's punishment, followed no better path. Though spared for a while because of the promising reforms led by one of her kings, Judah obstinately chose the path

to destruction. God sent Babylon to conquer the nation though He spared a remnant (2 Kings 25:8-30). It would be 70 long years before Babylonian captivity would end. It would be another 58 years (458 BC) before Ezra would engage in his mission.

The opening of Ezra's book begins with a capture of God's sovereignty. It was the Lord who rose of Babylon to conquer Judah in an act of divine judgment. It was the Lord who took away power from Babylon and gave it to the Medo-Persian Empire. It is the Lord who continues to engage in the world's affairs (Acts 17:26-28).

At Cyrus's decree, a contingent of Jews taken by Babylon began their trek back to Jerusalem (Ezra 1:1-11). From his own account, Ezra was not among this first group. This initial group was led by Sheshbazzar, who was the son of Judah's former king, Jehoiachin (2 Kings 24:13-16; 25:27-30; Jeremiah 52:31-34). The more prominent leader of this group of returnees was Zerubbabel, who some scholars recognize as Jehoiachin's grandson.

The initial contingent of returnees arrived in Jerusalem and began to build an altar for worship. They restored the worship of the Lord with the sacrifices that God had commanded through Moses (Ezra 3:1-7). Afterward, they began the work of rebuilding the temple (Ezra 3:8-13). This was no easy task, yet the people were determined to accomplish it. When the foundation of the temple had been laid, there was a mixed reaction from the returnees. While many shouted in praise of thanksgiving, some of the older returnees—those that remembered the majestic nature of the first temple—wept. These were overcome by the memories of what they had lost in comparison to the smaller temple they now saw.

The promising start to rebuild the temple soon met with resistance from some of the newer inhabitants of Jerusalem. These were the people who had populated the area as the result of Assyria's takeover of Israel. The Assyrians' practice in conquest was to deport most of the inhabitants of a conquered territory and to import other peoples into the newly conquered lands. Some Jews from conquered Israel were left in the area. These

Chapter Eleven

intermarried with imported peoples. This is the origin of the Samaritan peoples, whom other Jews considered to be a mongrel group. This resultant hatred is portrayed quite vividly in the time of Jesus on earth. A contingent of these racially and culturally mixed Jews had been living in Jerusalem when the Babylonian captives returned (Ezra 4:1-2).

Because they were denied joining in the restoration effort, Samaritans and other forcefully migrated peoples began doing all that they could to frustrate the rebuilding of the temple. Their protest was strong, and they received support from the new regime of the Medo-Persian empire to halt the temple rebuilding project (Ezra 4:6-24). From the initial return of the exiles (538 BC) by edict of Persian King Cyrus (ruled from 559-530 BC), through the reigns of Cambyses (ruled from 530-522 BC), and Darius (ruled from 522-486 BC), the returned exiles faced continuous opposition to the rebuilding of the temple. For a period, the building project stalled and stopped, and the people shifted their attention to rebuilding their individual lives. God sent the prophets Haggai and Zechariah to stir the people's spirits to resume and complete the rebuilding of the temple (Ezra 5:1-3; Haggai 1:1-15). Finally, after much opposition and some procrastination, the temple was completed (515 BC): a 23-year project (Ezra 6:15-18).

Ezra's account informs us that he came back to Jerusalem during the reign of Persian King Artaxerxes (also known as Longimanus—ruled from 464-423 BC). Fifty years had elapsed between the end of chapter 6 and the beginning of chapter 7 in the Book of Ezra. Eighty years had passed since the first exiles had returned. The worship of the God of Israel had been resumed with the various sacrificial offerings prescribed by Moses (Ezra 6:13-22). Ezra was the product of priestly lineage, and his return would mean great things for the restoration of God's worship (Ezra 7:1-5). He had a clear purpose in mind with regard to God's worship, and it involved seeking, doing, and teaching the Lord's commandments (Ezra 7:10). With astounding favor from the Persian king, Ezra set out to fulfill his mission (Ezra 7:11-28).

Lessons for Worship

Ezra's mission in traveling back to Jerusalem was filled with challenge and intrigue. Thankfully, he did not shrink from the task. In doing so, he left us with lasting lessons concerning worship. These lessons are summed in his stated purpose (Ezra 7:10).

If worship has to do with anything, it has to do with the condition of our hearts. This is first and foremost because it dictates all other elements of worship. Throughout the Old Testament, there is tremendous emphasis placed upon the condition of the heart (Leviticus 19:17; Deuteronomy 4:29; 6:5-6; 30:6; Psalm 139:23; Jeremiah 17:10). Jesus re-emphasized this matter during His earthly ministry (Matthew 5:8; 12:34-35; Mark 7:6-7).

The heart must be prepared for worship. This is something that must be done long before we enter into an assembly or even a time of private devotional. Some Christians and churches tend to place much emphasis on perfecting the worship rituals but spend little time on preparing their hearts. The Lord wants us to come to Him with sincerity of mind and purpose. Ezra prepared his heart, and we must do the same.

Ezra did not prepare his heart without purpose. He readied his heart to seek after God's law for his life. He devoted himself to searching out the Lord's Word and way of life. This is an element of worship that is too often forgotten or dismissed.

There can be no genuine worship without a burning desire to hear God's Word. This is powerfully apparent when we consider what God's Word means to us. First, we cannot know anything about the object of our worship without His revealing Himself to us. The Lord principally reveals Himself to us via the Scriptures. Admittedly, there are some things that we can know about God via His creation. Paul proclaimed that the heathen world could know some elemental things about the Lord by observing the very world that He created (Romans 1:18-23). Certainly, humanity could recognize that the Creator of all could not be made by His creation. The apostle made use of similar logic in preaching to those philosophers he encountered in ancient

Chapter Eleven

Athens (Acts 17:26-28). Further, God's creation gives reason for understanding proper natural relationships between males and females (Romans 1:24-27). Only corrupt and depraved minds can ignore what is natural and supplant it with the unnatural. In short, we can know something about the nature of God by means of His creation. However, God is chiefly revealed in the Scriptures.

No Christian can minimize or dismiss the essential primacy of God's Word in worship. To do so can and will lead to false worship. This is the inherent danger in attempting to design our worship around attractive music, sensory-appealing atmospheres, and emotionally titillating experiences. Perfecting each of these areas will not necessarily draw people into a relationship with the God of heaven. In many cases, the opposite is true. People can become attracted to our music and our technologically enhanced atmosphere at the expense of actually learning the gospel of Christ. People can become deceived and entrenched in believing things about the Lord that are not revealed in His Word. The result will be a clichéd Christianity that provides a dusting of truth covering the deep ground of worldliness. Sadly, many are accepting philosophical ideas dressed as Christian teaching. Such ideas can go undetected when our senses are dulled by the theatrics of modern-day "worship experiences."

It is the Word that teaches us of God, His nature, and His will for us. Songs, prayers, and praises must be in agreement with the Word and not mere pseudo-conversions of philosophical ideas, worldly concepts, and religious practices. We cannot honor the Lord in worship when we have no scriptural sense of who He is and what He commands.

The place of the Scriptures in worship must be paramount. From Nehemiah's account of Ezra's worship leadership, God's Word was read and explained thoroughly (Nehemiah 8:1-8). This was no casual attitude concerning the Word. This was no mere 10-minute add-on placed in between sessions of exuberant praises. This is especially striking when we remember the situation of these former exiles. They had been away from their land for decades. They had been captives in a foreign land for so long that many chose not to go back. Those who did return did so under great risk. Now, they had rebuilt the temple and resumed God's worship. If anyone had a reason to major in exuberant praise and minor in hearing the Word, it was they. However, the Word was central to their worship. Ezra and others made a deliberate and prepared effort to ensure that the people understood the written revelation of the God of Israel.

It is incumbent for church leaders to promote and maintain the primacy of the Word in corporate worship. Sadly, we are living in a time of increasing Bible illiteracy. Ironically, this is occurring in a time in which technology has made the Bible more available than ever before. Our corporate worship should not be designed to promote more praise and less preaching. It is the gospel that saves. It is God's Word that feeds the soul and lightens the path. Yes, the church needs to praise the Lord to the highest. Yes, songs of praise contribute to our knowledge of the Word. However, songs of praise must be centered in God's Word. They must be informed by God's Word. They are designed to reinforce the Word upon our souls, not to send us into a pseudo-spiritual trance. Songs, prayers, preaching, and praise must all be centered in God's Word.

Another lesson for worship from Ezra is the need to live the Word. He prepared his heart to seek out God's commands and to put them into practice. For him, it was not enough to hear the Lord. He knew that the Lord must be obeyed as well. Nor was this a lesson easily learned. Years of captivity after the bitter takeover by Babylon were experienced because of disobedience. Historians' description of Jerusalem's fall paint an indelible picture of the tragic events. The prophet Jeremiah, in addressing this sorrowful event, spoke of starvation in the sieged city and mothers eating their babies (Lamentations 2:19-20; 4:4-10). Those who understood this to be the pouring out of God's wrath on disobedience would doubtless have fixed the need for obedience deep in their hearts. Surely Ezra had done so.

Chapter Eleven

Worship is not completed when we sing praises and hear from God's Word. Far from this, worship must involve dedication to following the Lord's commands and instructions for life. Our Lord emphasized this need during His earthly ministry (Matthew 7:21). God is not interested in people praising Him with their lips while ignoring Him in their living.

It is important to remember that a heart of obedience to the Lord is not a life of perfection before the Lord. We have not been called to perfection. We have been called to be disciples, followers, and imitators of Christ Jesus. Often, Christians become quite pharisaical in these matters. We tend to develop our own standards of right and wrong behaviors and practices. We consider these to be the standard of perfection. We then want to hold others to these standards and condemn them when they do not. Sadly, much of what we develop is based in our own racial, cultural, and traditional mores. Like Pharisees in the time of Jesus, we often talk loud, but our lives say little.

We do well to develop a perfect heart before the Lord. This is one where we passionately seek to live for Him, and we humbly acknowledge when we fail to do so. It is a life of confession in the continuous process of seeking to draw closer to Him (1 John 1:8—2:2). As we live in this manner, we foster even more of an obedient heart. The grace of God that extends forgiveness to us for our failures ignites the heart with a deeper love for Him. Obedience is the loving response to the gracious pardon granted to us. Ezra well knew his people's sin and God's resultant righteous judgment. He also understood God's mercy in Israel's allowance to return to their land. His clear purpose was to exhort the returnees to obedience.

There is one final lesson for worship gained from Ezra. He dedicated himself to teaching God's law to the people. As we read the remainder of Ezra's account, we can see the meticulous nature in which he led the people in their worship and in their lives. He sought to leave no stone unturned in teaching God's ordinances. Ezra sought to learn God's way, to practice God's way, and to teach others of God's way. This the true pattern of worship.

Drawing Nearer

When we consider the commission that we have as Christians, we must understand the wisdom of Ezra's pattern. Jesus calls us to go and make disciples. Of course, this requires teaching others about Him. However, people will only hear us with our words when they have heard us with our deeds. As we live our lives in agreement with God's Word, people will open their ears to our words. Countless individuals have turned a deaf ear to Christian verbal testimony because of observed deficiencies in Christian behavior. This does not mean that we should never seek to teach others the gospel until we have reached perfection. If we did that, then we would never be able to speak the gospel to anyone. However, it does mean that we must strive to present a consistent, authentic Christian life-witness in the world. Our family, friends, neighbors, co-workers, and relative strangers must see us as people genuinely seeking to live what we say we believe. Nothing creates a receptive ear like an authentic witness.

Ezra sought to teach God's commands to Israel. The people's waywardness had caused them to forget the manner of life into which they had been called by covenant. These were not first-generation, former Egyptian slaves. Hundreds of years had past since God had given His law through Moses. Yet— God's law had never changed, so His people needed to be called to understand what most had never known.

Church leaders, preachers, and teachers have a special charge to instruct God's people in the Word. Clearly, we are living in a time of unprecedented ignorance of the Scriptures. Many Christians spend very little time in the Word. Those with the task of instructing the church must put forth maximum effort to faithfully teach the Scriptures. A church without the knowledge of the Scriptures is a church heading for apostasy.

Teaching the Scriptures is not just limited to Christian audiences. We are called on to teach the gospel of Christ to everyone (Mark 16:15-16). This is incumbent upon all Christians. Our commission is to teach others the good news of the salvation through Christ Jesus. For our non-Christian friends and neighbors, this means taking advantage of opportunities to talk

Chapter Eleven

about Jesus, to tell them who He is, and to relay what God has done through Him for our salvation. A loving and patient series of conversations about this can lead to someone giving himself to the Lord in baptism. A life-witness becomes a critical factor in the conversion process.

Final Thoughts

Ezra was quite a man. His story presents us with the full picture of worship. He takes us out of the routine of mere ritual and shows us the need for a prepared heart. He pushes us out of the realm of mere emotional praise and forces us to see the vital need of God's Word. He confronts us with the demand to learn and to do what God commands. He reminds us that the witness of our lives is crucial to the acceptance of our testimony.

May Ezra's example remain with us whenever we gather for worship as God's church as well as when we privately worship Him as one of His adopted spiritual children.

For Further Thought

1. Why is the condition of our heart so important to God?
2. How do we develop a heart for God?
3. What is meant by the primacy of Scripture in worship?
4. Why must the Bible be paramount in our worship?
5. What are the dangers of seeking to create an atmosphere for worship?
6. Why is it important to live a life of confession?
7. What is the connection between a life-witness and a life of confession?
8. How does a life of confession help us with evangelism?

Drawing Nearer

Chapter Twelve

My Personal Preparation for Worship

Introduction

These Old Testament characters have much to say to us about worship. The mindsets they held, the approaches they took, and the ways in which they expressed themselves present a mirror for us to consider how we worship. In this final section, we take a look at how we can develop a personal worship life that contributes to the beauty of the corporate worship experience.

Daily Reading and Meditation

If you are not a person who spends time reading the Bible or even knows how to go about reading it, you are not alone. You are among the majority of Christ-followers. This is quite a different era for the church. Like the rest of the population, Christians are caught up in the tyranny of the urgent.

Drawing Nearer

I remember attending a high school graduation sometime in the mid-1980s. During the commencement address, the speaker said that we were entering the "age of information." He could not have been more correct. Today, information on any topic is at the tip of our fingers. Access to various ways of reading or hearing the Bible is no exception. However, many Christians have no idea of where to start and how to go about feeding themselves on God's Word. It is of little wonder why we can struggle to have the corporate worship experience that our souls desire.

We must remember that the Bible is somewhat like a library. When we go into a library, we walk into a treasure trove of information. There are biographies, autobiographies, histories, sciences, arts, mathematics, and a host of other areas of learning. We normally select an area of interest and then sort through the library to get the books or articles that suit our needs. In a similar sense, this is how we can approach our personal reading of the Bible.

God's Word houses eternal treasures. We learn who He is. We learn who we are. We learn how we came to be. We learn of God's dealings with humanity. The Bible is the book of books lighting the path to eternal life. How then do we approach it and develop a daily reading and meditation habit? Here are three suggested approaches.

Study by Book or Letter

A book or letter study provides the advantage of grasping a more comprehensive reading of the Scriptures within a specific context. This kind of study lends itself to proving a richer understanding of and appreciation for God's Word among a particular community of people. We can often find ourselves among these communities in terms of our thoughts, concerns, struggles, and needs. All this prepares us for approaching the Lord in worship.

There are useful tools to assist us in approaching the Bible by a book or letter of the Bible. These tools include study Bibles, Bible dictionaries, expository Bible dictionaries, and lexicons. The

Chapter Twelve

value of these tools is found in their contribution to our overall understanding of our reading. Study Bibles provide us with such information as the background of a book or letter that we are reading. Bible dictionaries further enhance this information by informing us of the issues that the book or letter addresses, what was going on at the time of the writing, and other related information. Expository Bible dictionaries provide detailed definitions of Hebrew, Aramaic, and Greek terms from which our English Bibles were translated. Lexicons provide an even deeper level of defining these terms.

To study the Bible in this manner, consider what area of which you are wanting to learn more. The "library" consists of sections on history, biography, autobiography, prophecy, and much more. Next, read an introduction to the book or letter to familiarize yourself with the content and context of the book or letter. Begin reading the book or letter. Set aside a time of day or night to patiently read. Read with an inquisitive mind, making notes about things into which you want to dig further. This kind of reading will develop a greater thirst for reading the Scriptures. Asking the Lord to increase your understanding as you continue to read will result in a heart-connection with Him that feeds into an experiential walk with Him. Your worship experience will be greatly enhanced the more your study of, meditation on, and practice of God's Word increases.

Study by Topic or Subject

Topical studies provide the benefit of gaining a more comprehensive knowledge of what God says regarding a specific topic or subject. The benefit of this helps us to appreciate a fuller understanding of God's message on the particular matter.

Two particular tools are helpful in this study approach. One tool is a topical Bible. This tool categorizes Bible texts by subject or topic. Subjects such as repentance, giving, love, and a host of others can be searched, and a collection of Bible texts on these subjects can be read. As you study these various texts, take notes on what each reveals. Write down questions you may have regarding what you read. These questions can be discussed with other Christians as a means of enhancing personal and group understandings of the Bible.

A study by topic can be particularly useful when the desire is to delve more deeply into something that interests you. There may be a unique area of struggle or concern about which you may want God's counsel. The wealth of information gained through topic or subject study can do more than increase our knowledge of what God says about a subject. It can also increase our sense of connectedness to the very songs we sing in worship.

Study by Character

A final suggested approach to the reading of the Bible is reading about particular characters and their interaction with the Lord. Perhaps this approach lends itself to the most intimate of Bible studies. The Scriptures are full of individuals grasping and groping for a better understanding of the Lord's way as they struggle with the various issues and circumstances of life.

Some of the best character studies can be found in the Old Testament. There we find people who are familiar with the struggles of trying to live a God-centered life in a Satan-dominated world. These persons are surrounded by the influences of their heathen communities as well as personal hardships among family and friends. They are tried in various ways, they slip, and they fall. Some fall never to get up while others show an amazing capacity for holding true to the God of heaven in spite of human frailty. In these characters we find personal connections that can lift us and carry our hopes for victory forward as we travel along our personal faith-walk. These make major contributions to our spiritual development. Their stories, enhanced by our use of a Bible dictionary article that helps flesh out the biblical account, develop a thirst within us to come back for more. These journeys with people of similar character and disposition help us to see ourselves in a new light, and all of this prepares us for times of prayer and praise.

Chapter Twelve

The Word, Our Lives, and Our Worship

As we close our thoughts on worship, I want to encourage you to see the comprehensive nature of this simple word. Worship is not a mere Sunday exercise wherein we make use of various external means that somehow get us into a spiritual mood. Musical enhancements, stage productions, and colorful lighting are not the essence of worship. Traditional songs and various ritual practices are really not the essence of worship either. These and related things are often promoted as ways for us to enhance our worship experience, but they can miss the core of what worship is all about.

Worship begins and ends with God. His revelation to us calls us to see Him for who He is. His dealings with humanity as revealed in His Word inform us of His mercy, goodness, and grace. His dealings with us as we seek a faithful response to His call upon our lives compose the story of our faith-walk. We feed on His Word, we struggle to live for Him, and we face the ups and downs of our faith-walk. In the midst of all this, we cry out to Him in pain, in perplexity, and in praise. As this happens in our times of personal and corporate worship, we come to a richer experience that brings us closer to Him.

Let this be your lifelong aspiration. Let your worship experience continually draw you nearer to Him. Let it make your walk with the Lord much dearer. Draw nearer to God, and He will draw near to you.

Notes

www.ingramcontent.com/pod-product-compliance
Lightning Source LLC
LaVergne TN
LVHW052258070426
835507LV00036B/3317